HIGH HALDEN
AT
WAR

Ed Adams

CANTERLEY
PUBLISHING

Published by Canterley Publishing
www.canterley.co.uk
info@canterley.co.uk

Printed in the United Kingdom.

ISBN-13: 978-1-7399928-2-8

First published 2021.

ACKNOWLEDGEMENTS

This book could not have been written without the aid of the following people, to whom I am grateful for their time and generosity:

Harold Apps, Chas Bell, Frank Bourne, Kim Buggins, Kelly Burlton, Lyn Day, Peter Deacon, Nora Ferris, Jack Gillett, Debbie Greaves, Nick Hudd, Bert Kingsnorth, Barbara McGurk, Hilary Millen, Lorna Millen, Richard Milton, Duncan Prebble, Sue Rose, Alister Smith and Pat Wenbourne.

For access to their historic holdings I thank the staff of the Kent History and Library Centre, Lambeth Palace Library, the Imperial War Museum and the National Archives.

I am indebted to Marcia Mitchell and Ian Murdoch, whose 1981 publication *High Halden: the Parish and the People* has been a constant companion. I also owe particular thanks to Katharine Ames-Lewis who allowed me access to the text of her great-aunt May Maurice's fascinating diary and correspondence.

Finally, I offer my most heartfelt thanks to my wife Frances, and my daughter Emily, who teaches me new things every day.

CONTENTS

PRELUDE

THE PARISH OF High Halden, in the Weald of Kent, has long been noted for its bucolic beauty and charm. Its bordering parishes spread out in the manner of a five-pointed star: Smarden to the north, Biddenden to the west, Tenterden to the south-west, Woodchurch to the south-east and Bethersden to the north-east. While its key artery is the Hastings to Canterbury road (today called the A28), and responsible for the shape and growth of the village centre, those who dismiss High Halden as a nondescript linear settlement along a busy main road surely do it an injustice: the wider parish boasts areas of beauty that match anywhere else in the Weald.

It is a parish made up of manors, quarters and hamlets, with today's village centre corresponding to that once known as Hathewolden, meaning 'Heathuweald's woodland pasture', giving the modern name with its -den suffix so evocative of this part of England and its Anglo-Saxon origins. That said, a Roman road – testament to an early, successful invasion – runs through one of its constituent manors, Tiffenden, which was significant enough to be listed in the Domesday survey. At the northern end of the parish, Middle Quarter and Further Quarter, lead to isolated farms and remote clusters of homesteads – it has been speculated that they bear a Continental influence, and that 'quarter' derives from the French *quartier*, a unit of land used mostly by the Huguenots.

In common with the surrounding villages, its main historical industry was agriculture for the wool and cloth trade, although an enterprise at Further Quarter gave its name to dwellings such as Potkiln Farm, Potteries Farm and Pottery Cottages. This industry began producing Halden Ware in the 1600s but by the early 20th century had ceased; its decline hastened by the cheaper mass-produced pottery that could be transported from larger centres of manufacturing by train. High Halden's own station opened in 1905 at the western extremity of the parish, linking to the London mainline at Headcorn to the north, and Tenterden and Robertsbridge (and from thence the coast) to the south. It was an immensely charming if hokey old rattler which barely ever scraped a profit, but provided a vital service to local farmers in transporting their goods to market.

The railway also provided early-20th century High Halden with one of its village characters: stationmaster Henry Cambridge, who had held this position since 1910. Cambridge and his wife lived in a little wooden bungalow adjacent to the station, and while on duty this 'elderly man with keen eyes and silvering moustache' would entertain the passengers with sentimental tunes on his beloved violin, which he claimed to be an original Stradivarius. His pursuit of culture extended to collecting precious glassware and rare first editions of books – but in doing so he may have neglected his duties as carter for the local farms. One correspondent teasingly called him a 'wily old dog' who used any excuse to avoid loading up her apples for transport.

High Halden's principal landowner during the 1930s was Constantine Voltos, a Greek businessman who owned Harbourne Hall – a Palladian-style mansion built in 1875 – and its estate, though spent much of his time in London or abroad. A rebellious attitude was evident from childhood. When enrolled at Clifton College in Bristol aged 16, he became the subject of the fastest-ever dismissal from that august institution, when he escaped on his first day and was expelled on his second. As the school's official history relates, 'Attempted escape could not in itself have justified expulsion, and it is hard to imagine how adequate mischief could have been wrought in so short a stay.' His reputation was (somewhat) restored by the Great War, in which he served in the Royal Artillery and worked as an interpreter.

Voltos was installed at Harbourne Hall shortly after the war, while still in his twenties, and it became the venue for some lavish hunting and shooting parties, regularly hosting the Ashford Valley Hounds and, at least twice, King George II and Queen Elisabeth of Greece – in 1925 and 1928, the time of their exile from the Second Hellenic Republic. These lofty connections did not impress the staff of Tenterden Rural District Council, to whom Voltos was perhaps their notorious late-payer of council rates. Court proceedings

were threatened on several occasions: the first time, he was
bailed out by a friend to the tune of £50; by the end of 1938
his arrears had risen again to £100, and still with seemingly
no appetite to pay them off.

At nearby Tiffenden Manor was Louis Miller, a theatre actor
better-known by the stage name Guy Mills. Taking after his
sister, the more famous screen actor Ruby Mills, he was to
branch into film after the war. His greatest successes,
however, were as a stunt double – a renowned horseman,
he stood in for Errol Flynn on several occasions. The minor
aristocracy were also represented in High Halden with the
Honourable Eveline Godley at Durrants Court, second
daughter of Lord Kilbracken, an Anglo-Irish baronet. She
was a sometime author, keen gardener and amateur
astronomer, and doyenne of High Halden's Women's
Institute. Also shortly to arrive in the parish, after his
marriage in Tenterden, was the Honourable Peter
Montefiore Samuel, son of the 2nd Viscount Bearsted and
grandson of the founder of Shell.

By far the most colourful and well-travelled character to call
High Halden home during these years was a gentleman
named Charles Welsh Mason. The son of a clergyman,
Mason grew up in Kent and had travelled to China in 1887
to work as a customs officer. Within a few years he had
attempted to fund, equip and train an armed rebellion
against the state, and served a twelve-month prison term for
smuggling arms. Mason was lucky: his Chinese collaborators

were all executed, a fact that caused him the only regret in his life. He embarked on a literary career in England, with stories based on his experiences in China published under a series of pseudonyms. Then he went to Canada to participate in the Klondike gold rush, lived alone on an island, married and had three children, settled in New York, established himself as a journalist, divorced his wife and went travelling again. Mason returned to Canada where he lived in a shack by the Hudson river. He came back to Europe to serve in the Great War – while in his fifties – and then went back across the Atlantic again where he undertook menial jobs in the States, including as a roadbuilder.

Around 1923, having decided to call an end to his adventuring, Mason came back to England for the last time. Nearing sixty, but with all of his youthful energy intact, he bought a plot of land next to Brook Wood on Plurenden Road and built for himself a small cabin, eight feet square. Mason was to live a hermit-like hand-to-mouth existence there for three decades: when he needed more space, he simply built another room. Within ten years it had expanded into a substantial and rambling pile with a curiously fairytale mixture of Gothic and Oriental influences including arched windows, Eastern turrets and battlements. The locals called it the 'Queer House'. He also fell foul of Tenterden Rural District Council for non-payment of rates; unlike Constantine Voltos, however, Mason was able to plead extreme poverty, and was usually treated sympathetically.

At a more local level, matters of specific consequence only to High Halden were handled by the parish council, made up of around ten councillors — all male, and one of whom, chairman William Martin, would serve for nearly three decades. They were largely drawn from farming, business or military backgrounds. Two of them — Charles Brown of Hales Place and Charles Buss of Brickyard Farm — also worked for Tenterden Rural District Council, then based at 5 East Hill, Tenterden. A past chairman, Charles Wright of Hookstead, also served as a magistrate on the Cranbrook bench and was thus often called upon to pass judgement against fellow villagers, which caused no little resentment.

The village policeman, Constable Arthur Day, was a well-known and respected figure. High Halden was a fairly quiet posting for him; there was the usual cluster of rural crimes such as poaching and opportunistic theft, and the occasional disturbance at the village pubs. PC Day's finest hour had been in September 1937, when he tracked down a lorry which, after some homemade cider at Bethersden and another few at the Chequers, had been drunkenly driven into a hedge, telegraph pole and another car on the way to Tenterden. Day followed the erratic tyre-tracks, caught up with the abandoned lorry and apprehended the three men staggering arm-in-arm further on.

The rector of the church of St Mary was Rev. Arthur Champion, born in Derbyshire and previously archdeacon of Sarawak in Malaysia. His travels, undertaken with his wife

Ruth, were spiritually broadening but had left a legacy of exotic ideas and unfortunate ailments – he suffered from a recurring tropical illness which flared up from time to time, the last attack in 1936 requiring several months' recuperation away from his duties at home. As to his views, since his arrival in 1934 the more rustic of his parishioners had been bemused to see candles and crosses appear on the altar and highly-decorative furnishings around the church walls. The children's corner of the church was provided with a statue of the Madonna and Child, and an aumbry (a wall receptacle for storing the consecrated host) was also installed, which the Archbishop of Canterbury was pleased to approve but worried about how it might be received. Some whispered that the rector's churchmanship was so 'high' as to be positively Anglo-Catholic.

All this might have been problematic, given that the Weald of Kent had for centuries been a heartland of religious dissent against the established Church of England. Nearby Smarden enjoyed a significant Baptist influence, and in 1886 – within the living memory of many – some individuals in High Halden had contributed to local riots against the hated tithe-payments to the Anglican church. An accusation was also made that Methodists were attempting to take control of the village school, leading to what was almost a fist-fight in the church on Harvest Sunday that same year. While the tithe had effectively been abolished in 1936, there remained a parochial division between Anglicans (generally conservative-leaning landowners) and non-conformists (liberal farmers and labourers), though the militancy had, for the most part, faded away in the intervening five decades. Methodists in High Halden attended the Chapel by the entrance of what is now Hopes Grove, which was served by a succession of visiting ministers including, on occasion, Rev. Wilfred Paradine Frost of Tenterden, the father of broadcaster David Frost.

A perennial problem for St Mary's was the lack of funds to keep the church fabric in good order. In 1937 substantial renovations had been made, which included a new window, the moving of the organ from the south to the north chapel, the provision of electricity for the first time, and – most urgently – the reinforcement of the tower. The bell-frame was weak and being shaken ever more by the movement of the bells, and this in turn was damaging the integrity of the tower. It took several months of expensive work to make the structure safe – though the bells were left for the time being – and this necessitated several fundraising drives in an attempt to reduce the church deficit. But the building remained uncomfortable, constantly damp and impossible to warm effectively with oil heaters.

These activities during 1937 – which included whist drives, jumble sales and a fete held at Hookstead – helped to fill out a year of events to mark the coronation of George VI. There had been a free celebratory tea for all residents, a sports day in the grounds of Hathewolden Grange, and a social evening in the Memorial Hall. 175 commemorative coronation mugs were sourced and presented to the children as a keepsake, and a huge bonfire – a long and well-established High Halden tradition – was set alight on the village green in celebration. This golden summer of peace would prove to be the last hurrah before the gathering storm finally broke two years later.

The parish was made up of over sixty farms and farmsteads, with agriculture being the primary industry. In 1938 it was reported that every single farmer in High Halden was a member of the National Farmers' Union, which was believed to be a unique circumstance in the locality. Of these farms, Constantine Voltos owned the largest area, with Harbourne and Tiffenden estates combined. The rest were overwhelmingly tenant farmers, with the exception of several old established family farms where the occupancy had fallen to widows or maiden daughters – such as Tanden (Mrs Ledger), Church Farm (Miss Hukins) and Lion Farm (Misses Stockwell). Something of an anomaly in this area was Miss (Frances) May Maurice, who had bought Old House Farm in Further Quarter with her brother in 1920; when he died of tuberculosis, she carried on farming alone.

Still more unusual – and shocking, if it had been generally known – was the position of Miss Maurice's neighbour Susan Jackson, of nearby Haffenden, whose life was full of secrets and tragedies. Born Susan Hibberd in Wiltshire in 1869, she became a housemaid in Kensington, London and then fell pregnant, aged 22 and unmarried. Within a few years she and her daughter Violet Maud were living with William Neal, a wealthy newspaper editor nearly thirty years her senior, whose surname she used despite never marrying him. This bohemian attitude rubbed off on Violet who became an artist and hurriedly married a chartered secretary, Daniel Cambridge, on finding herself pregnant with his son William, who was born in 1913.

When war broke out the following year Violet developed extreme anxiety and would be paralysed with fear at the mere mention of a Zeppelin airship. In addition, after the birth of the couple's daughter Susan Mary in April 1916 she developed what we now understand to be postnatal depression, then known as 'puerperal insanity.' Susan was found dead at nine weeks old; suspicious of the circumstances, the police arrested Violet and at her trial in July she was found to have strangled the child, though was 'not responsible for her act at the time it was committed.' She was sent to Holloway Prison and released some months later after completing a course of treatment. By the end of the war she had gained the elevated position of Assistant Controller at Selfridge's in London. Violet became an athlete of some note, and was appointed President of the Women's Amateur Athletics Association. Her marriage to Daniel Cambridge ended in 1928 due to multiple infidelities on his part; this unhappy period coinciding with her appointment as manageress of the Elizabeth Arden beauty salon in Bond Street, where she was in charge of 80 staff. Violet – now known as Diana – then met and married Leslie Edwin Gordon Wall, a former officer in the Grenadier Guards now working as a writer and editor, in 1929.

Over the next ten years later Diana's mother Susan married and then became widowed from John Jackson, an English emigrant to far-off Flinders Island, Tasmania. She then settled at Haffenden, gaining many friends in the parish, becoming active in the Girls' Friendly Society and giving regular talks on the moral aspect of the organisation. Her daughter and son-in-law were frequent visitors and, while they were devoted to each other, Leslie preferred to remain at Haffenden with his mother-in-law, while the ties of her various positions kept Diana in London during the week. Mrs Jackson was proud of her daughter's achievements and her high standing in London was the talk of the village – Miss Maurice referred to her privately, and perhaps a little irreverently, as 'Elizabeth Arden.'

Outside of farming, the largest single employer in the parish was, and would be for some years to come, Woodgate's building firm. Established in the mid-Victorian era and fulfilling the associated role of undertaker in its early days, the company expanded greatly during the inter-war years under the energetic control of chairman William Peters Woodgate. As the need for social housing increased, Woodgate's won many contracts with Tenterden and Cranbrook Rural District Councils, including the 24 original

•

houses of the Hookstead estate in High Halden, built in two stages: 1928 and 1937. In 1938 alone they undertook two high-profile Cranbrook jobs: the building of a new cinema, and a huge reservoir at Hartley for the Cranbrook and District Water Company. The company now employed nearly thirty staff, and was all based on land extending behind William Woodgate's family home, Summerhill, between Hathewolden Grange and the Chequers.

Other trades included a wooden sign maker (Gilbert Horace), boot repairer (Thomas Herriott), tailor (William Hodgson) and butcher (Leslie Beale). George Robinson had the Auto-Service Station, on the site later occupied by Moriarty's, then US Cop Cars and now marked for development as Bishop Close. There was also a forge, opposite Woodgate's, with Bill Packham the blacksmith – a man renowned for his resourcefulness and skill that won him several prizes at agricultural shows. This obvious talent didn't stop chancers offering him 'payment in kind' for his work, which compelled him to display a sign stating I.B.F.C – 'I bash for cash.' Sadly he suffered from ill-health and died in 1939 aged 47; the village's last smith.

Two general stores served High Halden. Today's store is the successor to John Rofe and Sons, otherwise known as Rofe's, established in 1832, which also housed the village post office. The other, adjoining the school, was Ledger's, named after its owner of thirty years, Francis Ledger. He was approaching retirement and was soon to sell the business, but it would remain known as Ledger's for years to come. With its bakery section it tended towards confectionery and fresh produce; Rofe's stocked more essential household supplies. There was another important difference, too: the Rofe family were Methodists, while the Ledgers were Anglican. But most people used both shops without distinction, most often buying goods from each.

For liquid refreshment, High Halden boasted two public houses. The Chequers, occupying a prime spot by the green, was run by George Button and his family, and due to its location was most popular with villagers. Out on the Biddenden Road was the Man of Kent, run by Edmund Milton since 1921, in which Henry Cambridge the stationmaster was a regular with his violin, and where labourers from the outlying farms and travellers along the Maidstone road made up the clientele. Close by was the Old Thatched Barn, a tea room and guest house run by Lieutenant James Hogg, a veteran of the Royal Army Service Corps.

Education had been provided at High Halden's village school since 1868, and in the mid-thirties was overseen by headmistress Miss Olive Rossiter, a formidably no-nonsense character who upheld very high standards and in her prime could terrify fully-grown ex-pupils with a glance. Strong women ran in the family – Miss Rossiter's sister was Edith Adams, who in 1937 was elected the first lady Mayor of Tenterden. Yet after a stable couple of decades under her care the school was in a rocky patch by the end of the 1930s: Miss Rossiter suffered an unspecified accident and some ill-health, the infants' class was attended to by a succession of supply teachers, and – like the church opposite to which it was allied – the finances were precarious in the extreme, with no cash whatsoever to fund some badly-needed repairs and an extension to the playground.

Before the National Health Service medical care was paid for privately, and most villagers were on the books of the practice run by Doctors Cole, Taylor-Jones, Gaskell and Bentall – based in Benenden, Tenterden, Woodchurch and Rolvenden respectively. There were a couple of medical practitioners in the village – Dr Raymond Ring at the Old Thatched Barn, and Lieutenant-Colonel Edmund Stanley of Thirfield, who had trained in the Indian Medical Service – and while they might be consulted in extreme circumstances, they were either retired or practised elsewhere. High Halden had no resident nurse, a situation that was unusual by this point in time, and this issue would resurface a few years later.

Endowed by a charitable request dating from 1696, the only property owned by the parish council for the benefit of its people was four acres of pastureland in Further Quarter known as Poorsfield, on which a cottage had been built in the early nineteenth century. From 1936 the land had been leased for cattle grazing to the Adams family of Further Quarter, of whom Young Sam Adams (named as such to avoid confusion with his father, also Sam) sub-let it to George Woodgate, a cousin of William Woodgate. Adams and Woodgate were neighbours – living at 2 and 3 Pottery Cottages, respectively – but this arrangement was to turn sour within a couple of years when Woodgate refused to vacate Poorsfield, and when the parish council found themselves unable to intervene, Young Sam threatened to settle the matter with his fists. At the time, this was the most talked-about conflict in the parish, but it would soon be superseded.

As with everywhere else in the country, High Halden's people watched with anxiety as the international situation deteriorated in the latter half of the 1930s. Adolf Hitler, leader of the National Socialist party, who gained the chancellorship of Germany in 1933 and total control as Führer the following year, resolved to reinvigorate his country after the perceived injustices of the post-1918 peace treaties and crushing depression of the ensuing Weimar Republic. He poured money into restarting German industries, revolutionised the transport system and encouraged all-encompassing social change that went down to the level of every German family. But these laudable aims hid a darker motive: territorial expansion to provide living space for a Greater Germany – in effect, the entire German-speaking population of Central Europe – peopled only by the purest Aryans whom Hitler and his party viewed as ethnically superior to all other races.

In the following years Hitler was to violate the terms of the peace one by one, and encroach upon territories he viewed as being ethnically German. He built up the armed forces, remilitarized the Rhineland on the French border in 1936, gave support to the Italian invasion of Abyssinia the same year, and to Franco's nationalists in the ongoing Spanish Civil War. By the beginning of 1938 it was clear to many in Britain that another war with Germany was more likely than not. Such a war would be far more destructive to Britain and to civilians generally than the last: Prime Minister Stanley Baldwin had warned about the possibility of 'total war' six years earlier, and his words still rang in many ears:

> *I think it is well also for the man in the street to realise that there is no power on earth that can protect him from being bombed. Whatever people may tell him, the bomber will always get through. The only defence is in offence, which means that you have to kill more women and children more quickly than the enemy if you want to save yourselves.*

It was against this background that a Joint Committee of Air Raid Precautions was set up in the first months of 1938. It covered Tenterden Borough and both Tenterden and Cranbrook Rural Districts: an area of about 200 square miles 'from Appledore to Goudhurst and Frittenden to Stone-in-Oxney,' with a population of 22,700. The Committee had the wide-ranging brief of keeping civilians safe from any kind of aerial attack. Principally, volunteers were required for the posts of air raid wardens, auxiliary firefighters to supplement the local fire brigade based at Tenterden, demolition and rescue parties, and motorcyclists, cyclists and runners to help augment the telephone service. Women were invited to register as first aid personnel, nurses and 'support workers' to provide refreshment and comfort to those who might be rendered homeless.

Gas was perceived to be the main threat, as it was anticipated that the Germans would use the same tactics on British civilians as they had used in the trenches. It was announced that, in the event of war, gas masks would be distributed free of charge to every citizen. In the meantime, each household was to select a 'refuge room' that could be made gas-proof, and issued with instructions on how to do this with Plasticine and tape.

William Woodgate was appointed Head Warden of High Halden, and he reported to Major E.A. Godfrey, who was in overall charge of the ARP operations for Tenterden and Cranbrook from a temporary headquarters at 21 Ashford Road, Tenterden (lately Jenners). But recruitment to the ARP was slow at first. There was a natural resistance to any strictures on day-to-day life, as well as suspicion towards those assuming authority. The organisation was also, at first, suffused with bureaucracy and in-fighting: at a meeting in March, the irascible bursar of Cranbrook School, Major Percy Robathan, accused other districts (that is, Tenterden) of attempting to poach Cranbrook's men and lorries for their own patrols. He was assured this was not the case.

The same meeting was picketed by the Peace Pledge Union, who opposed conscription and the passing of laws for air raid precautions. Their local members handed out leaflets which starkly warned of the dangers if a peaceful solution was not sought:

> *[A gas-proof room] will keep the gas out for four or five hours, but as gas may remain outside for a week or more, the best you can expect is that you will die quietly at home.*

A legacy of the Great War of twenty years previously was that High Halden was full of veterans – several of whom were commissioned officers. In 1938 the parish boasted at least two majors, three captains, a lieutenant-colonel and a lieutenant-commander. Most of these men were retired from the forces. Others, such as Captain Ronald Fitz-Jenyns (late of the Royal Flying Corps) and the previously-mentioned Lieutenant James Hogg (Royal Army Service Corps) now pursued other careers – as a fruit grower and a tea-room manager, respectively. But all had the required experience, authority, and sheer determination to put up a decent fight, if the need should arise.

In April a pubic meeting was held at the Memorial Hall on the subject of Air Raid Precautions. Despite this, some were not unduly worried. Rev. Champion refused to believe that all hope was lost:

> *There is no reason for complacency... nor for neglecting elementary precautions against dangers which only a lunatic could ignore... but in any case I think it is a great mistake to think or to speak as though we were on the verge of a devastating European war.*

Many saw more pressing matters closer to home, such as the continued plight of farmers against low prices and the perceived lack of government support. Sydney Read of Little Robhurst Farm commented at a National Farmers' Union meeting in May that the government was 'more interested in gun fodder than human fodder.'

By now Germany had annexed Austria, the closest bordering country with the most 'ethnic Germans,' and with the support of the majority of Austrians who saw the Nazi regime as a robust alternative to their own weak government. Throughout the spring and summer of 1938 Nazis living in the Sudetenland rose up in agitation, demanding the autonomy of their region and its alignment with Germany. Hitler – who had most likely engineered the situation – threatened an invasion of Czechoslovakia if their demands were not met, and the crisis came to a head in September. Britain and France advised appeasement as the only way to avoid war; Hitler saw his opponents' weakness for what it was, and took advantage. Self-determination for the Sudetenland was no longer enough. He now demanded the complete annexation of the region into Greater Germany, with a view to the total dismantling of Czechoslovakia, which had been forged in the hated 1919 Treaty of Versailles.

War now seemed inevitable and Britain, it seemed, despite the warnings of Winston Churchill, had been caught napping. The might and efficiency of the German military had been amply demonstrated in Europe but there was very little in the way of emergency planning for what would surely be an immediate retaliation. Like everywhere else, High Halden scrambled hastily into preparations. Tenterden's fire service, intended to cover the entirety of the Borough and Rural District, now seemed hopelessly underequipped. But recruitment to the ARP, after the initial apathy, jumped to over 700 members. Gas masks, which had been secretly manufactured over the past year, began to be distributed.

On Saturday 24th September Rev. Champion wrote:

> *The international situation, as I write, is full of menace, and events are moving so rapidly that any detailed comment is impossible, even if I wished to make it. The need for prayer is regular and constant, and we must wait steadfastly upon God.*

Events were indeed moving quickly. Five days later Britain and France, mollified by Hitler's assurance that it was his last territorial demand in Europe, gave up the Sudetenland to him, and Neville Chamberlain returned from Munich the following day declaring 'peace for our time'. But the volunteers were not stood down, and continued to remain on the alert. With the Allies having failed to bring Hitler to heel, war had not been averted – simply postponed.

1939

SHORTLY AFTER THE Munich crisis of September 1938 the authorities realised that, had war been declared, they would have been woefully underprepared with regard to the evacuation of children and vulnerable adults out of areas likely to be bombed. Thus in January 1939 preparations began in earnest, with a preliminary letter to each household in the parish, followed up by a personal visit, with a view to drawing up a list of those willing to take in an evacuee or evacuees, should the need arise. This survey was complete by the end of February and, while it did not always meet with a positive response, records show that the people of High Halden were by and large willing to help.

Tenterden Rural District was earmarked to receive 820 evacuees a day over three days; 2,460 in total. Half would be reckoned to be schoolchildren; the rest, mothers, very young children and school staff. The single-track branch line on which High Halden's own station lay was judged insufficient to cope with the operation's demands, so the passengers would disembark from mainline stations. Despite the argument that Appledore was more conveniently placed for the southern and eastern parts of the district, Headcorn was chosen as the point for transferring to buses. There would be three special trains each day, arriving at Headcorn at 12.48pm, 3.20pm and 6.04pm: the last of these, from Grove Park, carrying those allocated to Biddenden and High Halden because they would have the shortest bus journeys. Of these evacuees, High Halden was to be allocated 324 in total, of which 150 would be unaccompanied children.

The appointed billeting officer for the parish was William Proctor, currently renting Harbourne Hall from Constantine Voltos. Proctor had led an interesting and eventful life but was a perhaps less than ideal choice for a position of such responsibility. Previously a jewellery dealer in Canada – where he had only narrowly escaped a devastating hotel fire in 1908 – by 1939 he was the retired managing director of a London manufacturing firm. In November 1924 he was stopped by police driving his car the wrong way down the Mall, and was charged with driving while drunk. Proctor's solicitor successfully argued that he had in fact been impaired by the chemical fumes in his factory, and that he had only taken 'two double brandies' to counteract the effect. The drunkenness charge was dismissed, but when Proctor was again stopped two months later driving erratically down Chelsea Embankment, it was incontestable. The judge sentenced him to one month's imprisonment and banned him from driving for two years.

The very fact that such a scheme was still being discussed put an end to the relief that had been enjoyed since the previous autumn. The public would have been even less heartened to know, for example, that in closed sessions Tenterden Rural District Council were discussing the fact that the council rate would be increased to cover the cost of civil defence, that oil and gas would be rationed, and that barns and similar farm buildings would be assessed to see whether they could be used as mortuaries to process the large number of civilian deaths that would surely follow. Little wonder that on 25th March Rev. Champion wrote that his people were 'feeling the strain with worry.' His wife Mrs Champion joined the Food Control Committee, along with Mr Brown (Hales Place) Mrs Musgrave (Hookstead Cottages) and Mr Proctor (Harbourne Hall) – another pointer towards the inevitable limiting of personal freedoms. This was widely anticipated, and at the WI's May meeting the Hon. Eveline Godley urged the members to start bottling and preserving fruit.

The Rector had worries of his own, too, as the state of the bell-frame in the tower now presented a critical danger to church-goers. The bells had now been silent for the best part of a year while the parochial church councillors argued over whether to repair the frame (cheaper, but likely to need more work in the short-term) or replace it entirely (expensive, but would last longer). In the end the latter option won the day, and Messrs Taylor of Loughborough – clearly worried how an impending war would affect their trade – offered a discount if they could get started immediately. Rev. Champion felt it would be more appropriate for them to show some faith, but the work was approved, and discussions on precisely how the beleaguered church might meet yet another expense were deferred for another day. It was against this frenetic background that the Bishop of Dover paid his pastoral visit to the church on 25th June.

A plucky counter-effort was also made to put worries aside, and for a few months this year High Halden featured in several light-hearted press stories to which reporters had been tipped off by local correspondents. There was mention of a cat belonging to Mrs Davis of Coombe View, who incubated hens' eggs by sitting on them – the cat, that is, not Mrs Davis. The name of Mr Weekes of Kirkbank Cottages cropped up with news of his four-foot scale model of *HMS Cairo*, which took two years to build from old cigarette packets and gramophone needles. The *Daily Mirror* ran a piece on Charles Welsh Mason, the hermit of whom many villagers were unaware, and brought his name to a national audience. The same paper also devoted several column inches to nine-year-old Byron Mercer, whose hair – kept in long ringlets and tied with blue ribbon – was causing a sensation at the school. The antics of Alfred Hukins of Old Place Farm – who took primitive aerial photographs by attaching a camera and timer to a kite – were also featured. (In these anxious times Mr Hukins was also liable to trigger a panic, by sending up dummy airmen whose parachute descent was triggered by the same timer.)

On Saturday 6th May the 385th Battery of the 97th (Kent Yeomanry) Field Regiment (then based at Canterbury, and under the command of Tenterden borough councillor Lieutenant-Colonel Franklin Lushington, but soon to move to Ashford) led a recruiting march through the Weald. Beginning at 2pm in Tenterden High Street, they proceeded to Biddenden, Benenden, Rolvenden, Wittersham, Appledore and Woodchurch, before arriving at High Halden – presumably rather tired – at 8.25pm. Their efforts were rewarded with a few hundred new recruits, and the unit would go on to play a significant role in future events in France.

Woodgate's – always busy – were finding themselves more in demand than ever, with new buildings required for the Tenterden ARP Committee, including a new Centre and Depot at Golden Square, Tenterden. In the end their tender for that project was not accepted, but they were luckier with the bigger job of supplying and fitting the necessary equipment in the Mobile First Aid units being established at Kench Hill (Tenterden), Hawkhurst Cottage Hospital and the Cranbrook Institution. The company kept good relations with the ARP committee and were generally their builders of choice, perhaps helped by William Woodgate's appointment as Officer in charge of Rescue Parties for the area. His responsibility would be to co-ordinate and muster mobile groups of workers to retrieve those trapped in bomb-damaged buildings – clearly a builder's experience was a great asset here, and Woodgate's employees made up the bulk of the roster.

But by June this great struggle that many were fearing had still not come, and there was a sense more of anticlimax than relief. Rev. Champion spoke of the lull in international affairs, reminding his people that war was not inevitable and that, in his opinion, the probabilities were against it. The only hint of conflict that broke into the open this summer was the ongoing one between Young Sam Adams and George Woodgate. A boundary dispute spilled over into violence when Adams accused Woodgate of stealing lilac from a tree, and the two men came to blows. Woodgate came off worse, receiving a wallop on the head with a stick. He summoned Adams to court for assault, but was himself cross-summonsed by Adams for the damage to the tree. Adams was bound over to keep the peace for two years, and both men were told to grow up and behave themselves.

International tensions rose and relations deteriorated in July, with Britain proving unable to persuade Soviet Russia to come on board as an ally. The British feared that if the Russians instead sided with Germany, Hitler and Stalin would be at liberty carve up Eastern Europe between them, precipitating the long-expected war which would be sparked, in all likelihood, in Poland.

Emergency procedure kicked in, in a similar vein to eleven months previously. A circular was addressed to all

•

householders in the Tenterden Rural District on 4th August, informing them of their parish emergency committees and announcing a forthcoming meeting to be held in each village from 18th August, which would be addressed by Charles Brown. The evacuation plan was put in a state of readiness, with the council writing to all village halls to ask if they could be converted into canteens – Rev. Champion is known to have written to the council on the issue of communal meals for evacuees, but the details are sadly unknown. Other issues relating to the evacuation plan, such as the refusal of some well-placed householders to take any, or the unsuitability of certain people to host children, were ironed out by Mrs Musgrave, who visited 'cases of difficulty' all over the district.

In a particularly local connection to the national efforts, Sir Auckland Geddes of Frensham Manor, Rolvenden Layne, was appointed Commissioner for Civil Defence for the South-East Region, under which brief he regularly visited the Tenterden district to see how preparations were going. His visits were morale-boosting and appreciated, though he often came away with private reservations as to how effective his measures might prove. His wife, Lady Geddes, also threw herself into voluntary schemes and was a very visible presence at women's meetings during these times.

To the surprise of most of the public, a non-aggression pact between Nazi Germany and Soviet Russia was signed on 24th August, and the fate of Eastern Europe was sealed. With the hope of avoiding war now disappearing, ARP units were given the order to 'stand ready' the following day.

Plans for both the blackout and the evacuation sparked into life. London families wishing to evacuate their children were told to make immediate preparations, and High Halden's school was cleared and prepared for their reception. Civilians were now told to dig out their year-old gas masks and gather their blackout material. Vehicle owners were told to mask their headlamps with a hood that directed the beam downwards towards the road.

On the evening of Monday 28th August, 'the most lovely summer night,' May Maurice of Old House Farm put pen to paper and began a diary to record her thoughts on the impending war and its progress. She would keep it going until the following April and, together with some correspondence which also survives, her words form an evocative account of life in the remotest part of the parish, particularly during the earliest months of the conflict.

Most of Miss Maurice's entries involve relations with her neighbours in Further Quarter. Her indefatigable helper on the farm was Mr Rootes, known as 'Toots', a dogged old retainer whose Eeyore-like pronouncements disguised a certain wisdom.

> *Toots opines Germany is 'better britched' than we thought — 'breeched' is 'trousered' and implies pockets too! He don't like to think of 'them Polands — doesn't*

*do to think these days,' he is sure. Shows his usual sense
in that, for if one does with Russia and Germany
trampling over Poland, one feels the power of evil.*

From Miss Maurice we also learn that a son of George
Burden at Pear Tree Farm has become a Special Constable
like his father, and that Muriel Hammond (Gates Farm) and
William McLeod (Dents Farm) are both air-raid wardens.
Over the next few weeks she would receive a telling-off
from all of them in turn for inadvertently 'showing a light'
after dark.

An emergency meeting was held at the Memorial Hall on the
evening of 31st August, chaired by Charles Brown of
Tenterden Rural District Council – with an apparent
Mainwaring-like bumptiousness that did not impress Miss
Maurice, who later wrote later 'Mr Brown [is] loving his
war.' She had spent most of the day making up beds for the
evacuees whom she expected to arrive the following day.

On the morning of Friday 1st September the government's
Executive Committee took control of the railways and at
lunchtime the first special evacuation train left from Hither
Green. The evacuees were met at Headcorn by members of
the Emergency Committee for Tenterden Rural District,
and placed on buses for the journey south. At 6.30pm the
first passengers for High Halden arrived at the school, were
given a hot drink and allocated to their hosts. Numbers were
nowhere near the 324 expected: overall, the district

received about a third of the 2,500 they had bargained for, so it is likely High Halden's total share was not much over 100. (Miss Maurice received none at Old House Farm.) Despite this, government support was slow off the mark: a blanket was supposed to be given for every two evacuees, but seven weeks later only half the required number had been supplied, making one to be shared between four. At the same time, the district was recorded to be 39 camp beds short of the total needed.

Most evacuees to the Tenterden Rural District under the official government scheme came from an area roughly south of Catford and north of Bromley, with particular clusters from Manor Lane and Church Street Schools in Lee. Enfield and Greenwich also sent a few children, as did Eltham – at least four of whom were Roman Catholic, having come from St Mary's RC School.

That same evening of their arrival, the lights were dimmed, masked, hooded, or just extinguished, all over Britain. This was the first night in the country for hundreds of displaced people, mostly children: in an unfamiliar home, without a bed, or a blanket; miserable, frightened, and in complete darkness. The next day, Tenterden's ARP Centre received the War Instruction telegram, meaning that conflict was expected imminently. Immediate action was taken to issue Civil Defence equipment, which was distributed to all wardens and volunteers through the night.

The following morning, Sunday 3rd September, a wireless announcement at 9am told listeners to tune in again at 10am. That deadline passed, and no word was given. Rev. Champion began Morning Prayer at 10.45am and then a well-attended Eucharist service at 11am – and still no news. While the service was underway, the Prime Minister finally addressed the nation at 11:15am:

> *I am speaking to you from the Cabinet Room at 10 Downing Street. This morning the British ambassador in Berlin handed the German government a final note stating that unless we heard from them by 11 o'clock that they were prepared at once to withdraw their troops from Poland, a state of war would exist between us. I have to tell you now that no such undertaking has been received, and that consequently this country is at war with Germany.*

The Rector is understood to have been passed a note, from which he announced the grave news from the pulpit, and invited the congregation to pray. The service continued, however, and the offertory that Sunday was significantly more generous – £4 2s 7d; roughly double the usual takings.

By an unfortunate quirk of timing, the work on the bell-frame was finished and the bells were once again ready to be rung that Sunday, for the first time in many months. An invitation had been sent to some bell-ringers from a neighbouring parish to come and try the new workings and share the celebration. In the end, though, the event was a disaster. Not only did the day's news cast a pall over the proceedings, with no-one certain how much longer ringing would be allowed, but the visiting ringers hogged the bells to such an extent that none of the locals were able to use them. Much to Rev. Champion's disgust, the interlopers then sneaked out of the church without attending the service. He wrote: 'This latter practice is wholly contrary to our traditions, and the whole incident was most regrettable.'

May Maurice had spent most of the day picking plums and making preserves to take her mind off the events:

> So ends a queer unreal day – one has felt as though one
> was in some tragic unreal play. Nothing seems real...
> one is just queerly tired that's all – must remember to
> eat properly. I've made 10 lbs of plum jam today.

Over the next month troops and armoured vehicles streamed through the village on their way to the coast. There was a movement for men to join up before they were conscripted – not a rush, like in the last war, but still a good proportion of High Halden's men in their late teens and twenties went to the recruiting office at Ashford. May Maurice tells of a 17-year-old neighbour whose boyfriend had joined the RAF, and the effect it was having on her:

> She was not going to believe in God anymore. [Her
> mother] remarked, 'Lot of hypocrisy.' It'd be interesting

to know how many [similar people] there are and if they offset the sort who war sends rushing to church (to appease the tribal god?). I can't feel very sympathetic with either…

Rev. Champion, who had seen it all before, had his own perspective on faith during wartime:

Sometimes such catastrophes have the effect of turning men's minds against God, much as a dog in pain may bite the hand of one who tends and feeds him.

Certainly suffering from a crisis of confidence in these early weeks were the evacuees – or, perhaps, their families – as many of them had evidently returned home by the end of the month. High Halden's school register shows that only eleven extra pupils joined the school roll when term began on Monday 2nd October, with another two following a few days later. Compared to Tenterden, where 375 extra children were squeezed into three schools (Tenterden CE School, Ashford Road Council School and St Michael's School) then it appears that High Halden was not overwhelmed by the extra demand. Nonetheless some of the evacuees that did come brought with them certain issues. These city children were handy with their fists, disdainful of the rustic ways of their hosts, and Frank Bourne remembered 'plenty of punch-ups, every day'. Miss Rossiter had no hesitation in caning the perpetrators, whatever their background.

Another problem was the spread of disease. 1939 had already seen a heavy outbreak of chicken-pox at the school, with twenty cases so far recorded in the first half of the year. Now the newcomers introduced the likes of impetigo and measles to the community, and cases weren't restricted to those at school, nor to Londoners. In September 18-year-old Eric Betts, originally from Hove, came to stay with the Back family at Chestnut House by the green. Shortly after his arrival he broke out in boils and was found to have scarlet fever. He was taken to Cranbrook Joint Hospital but died soon afterwards from a blood infection; a consequence of the boils turning septic. The medical authorities conducted a thorough investigation and discovered that he had contracted the illness in Hove, and had passed on some mild cases to a family in St Leonard's before coming to High Halden. Luckily for the village, the outbreak was successfully contained.

In 1939 Britain was importing the majority of its food: half of its meat; three-quarters of its sugar and cheese; 80% of its fruit (yes, even for Kent); and 90% of its fats and cereals. The people had been warned that, in a time of war, the supply of these products would be severely disrupted and that they should expect them to be rationed. On 29th September a national census was taken by John Rofe. (The job of enumerator had been done by a John Rofe in High Halden ever since the first national census of 1841.) The information from this exercise was used to issue identity cards and ration books over the coming months. For the villages of Tenterden Rural District, this was to be administered from 16th October by a National Registration and Food Office established at the council headquarters at 5 East Hill, Tenterden, and ration books were issued from this address.

Anyone who sold food to the public now had to register for a licence as a 'retail dealer,' and this rule applied equally to the smallest farms (selling butter, eggs, milk or fruit) as it did to the general stores. The Food Office was inundated with applications, all the way down to farmers with an honesty stall of eggs by the road, and by the end of the year High Halden accounted for 27 separate licences. Ledger's and Rofe's stores were granted separate licences to supply bacon and ham, and catering establishments (the Chequers, the Old Thatched Barn) were also granted the ability to obtain extra rations for their guests.

There were more rules to follow in wartime, particularly with regard to the blackout and associated precautions, and many otherwise law-abiding citizens fell foul of them. May Maurice was particularly accident-prone in this regard:

> *Nov 12. My perfect Sunday peace wrecked by a visit from [William] McCleod (air warden) to say last night he saw light streaming from my window – hardly can believe it but one doesn't argue with Air Raid Wardens*

> *so I have spent all my peace re-lining and re-hanging*
> *curtains.*

A more serious transgressor was William Proctor, who had continued his uneasy relationship with motor regulations: in November he was fined £1 for driving a car with an unscreened fog-light at Hurst Green. Barely three weeks later, he died suddenly of a stroke, and Rev. Champion took over his duties as billeting officer.

No explicit instruction has survived to confirm it, but anecdotal evidence suggests that High Halden's Memorial Hall had by now been earmarked as the parish mortuary, and was in the process of being fitted up to receive the bodies that many feared would accumulate. The authorities were aware, however, many such village halls would lose rental income through being unavailable to users. To counteract this, Tenterden Rural District Council asked for the organised collection of waste paper in every parish, which would then be sold to processing plants for recycling, and this small income put back into the village halls. It was the beginning of the salvage movement that was to endure throughout the war (and beyond), and the waste paper operation relied on much good work from the Boy Scout and Girl Guide Associations. The WI also did their part, appealing for salvage in their November meeting as well as giving 'a practical demonstration on making soap from waste fat.'

This period has been nicknamed the 'Phoney War' for good reason – despite much domestic activity in preparation, and plenty of personal restrictions, virtually none of the enemy activity in Europe impacted upon those at home. To some extent this was compounded by the fear of a knockout blow in early September which never materialised, and by December it seemed that the talk of heavy casualties and mortuaries from a few months previously appeared to have been just scaremongering. Consequently, and understandably, many people let their guard drop. The few remaining evacuees mostly returned home for Christmas – even fewer would return to the parish.

But in the last few weeks of 1939 there were a couple of pointers in High Halden as to the way things would be going. The first was the presence, from around late November, of soldiers in the grounds of Tiffenden Manor. Details are sparse, but it is known that at the end of the month a collection of gifts and money for their benefit was being organised by Mrs Champion. The hope was to assemble a huge hamper of food, gifts, cake and cigarettes to be sent to 'the Tiffenden camp' at Christmas.

Then came the village's first military casualty of the war. **Stoker George Albert Sutton**, aged 26, had been born in High Halden but moved away with his parents to Chatham during his childhood. He had been a career sailor for four years when war broke out, beginning service on the destroyer *HMS Bulldog*. Sutton was disappointed to be reassigned to the light cruiser *HMS Cornwall* in 1937, and two years later requested a transfer to the destroyer *HMS Duchess*.

At the outbreak of war *HMS Duchess* was sent to the Mediterranean, where it spent two months. Then in December it was assigned, with three others, to escort the battleship *HMS Barham* back to the United Kingdom. In heavy fog on the morning of Tuesday 12th December, *Barham* and *Duchess* collided off the Mull of Kintyre. *Duchess* capsized, setting off her depth charges in a series of huge explosions, and killing 136 of her crew, including Sutton.

Those who remembered the Sutton family were saddened when the news reached High Halden a few days before Christmas. Then came another blow, when on Saturday 23rd December, George Button, the much-respected landlord of the Chequers, also died from cirrhosis of the liver. Two sudden deaths, in the midst of life, and yet still no enemy in sight. It was a bitter foretaste of what was to come.

1940

THAT MOST TUMULTUOUS year in our recent history, 1940, began with disruption. On top of the continuing blackout and the fresh memory of recent and sudden bereavements over Christmas, heavy snow in the first few weeks of the year brought rural life to a literal standstill, and a persistent winter virus cut a swathe through the neighbourhood. Rationing was introduced on Monday 8th January, starting with sugar, butter, bacon and ham. Meat as a whole would be rationed a few weeks later, to the value of 1s 10d per person per week. This truly was a winter of discontent, but as Rev. Champion reminded his parishioners, 'Our actual tribulations are small compared to what millions in Europe and in the world are suffering.'

An ARP training exercise for all units took place at Sissinghurst on Sunday 25th February. This was followed by a whole-scale inspection of gas masks by the air-raid wardens, in advance of the deadline of Monday 8th April, after which any damage or loss would need to be paid for by the individual. Fortunately most of the equipment had survived intact. But as winter turned to spring and still no enemy action materialised, a little resentment grew up around these well-meaning officials and their rules.

One person finding himself at odds with the authorities was Charles Welsh Mason, who in March was summoned to attend Cranbrook magistrates' court for the non-payment of 18 shillings' council rates. He did not turn up to court, but instead sent a photograph of himself and a letter pleading intense poverty. He was already £4 in debt to his grocer and had been obliged to half-starve himself over the winter in consequence. His furniture belonged to his daughter, he explained, so instead of them being seized by a bailiff he offered to serve a prison term in lieu of payment. The magistrates were intrigued but not impressed, and ordered him to pay up.

The following month, Germany invaded Norway and so abruptly stopped the Scandinavian supply of wood pulp to Britain. This began the first major salvage drive, described as 'vitally important,' comprising of waste paper, cardboard and rags – all of which could be recycled and fashioned into paper. Each parish was instructed to make a place available for the deposit of waste materials. In High Halden a central spot was chosen near Lion Farm, and the collection began to accumulate.

By the time this was put in place, the international situation had deteriorated further. On Friday 10th May, Germany invaded Belgium and the Netherlands, forcing Chamberlain's resignation and Winston Churchill's elevation to Prime Minster. The speed and efficiency of the German *blitzkrieg* ('lightning war') was like nothing ever seen before, with the British Expeditionary Force encircled and driven back to the Channel coast. At Dunkirk they awaited rescue, which started slowly, with British destroyers constantly harassed by the Luftwaffe.

On Monday 27th May, one day into the Dunkirk evacuation, and with no sign that it would turn out to anything but a humiliating disaster, Rev. Champion sat down in his study and wrote his monthly pastoral letter to his flock, which ended as follows:

> *Finally, my dear people, I commend you to God. Keep a good courage. Don't give heed to rumours. Don't let your imagination run away with you. And be thankful to God for many encouragements.*

The miracle of Dunkirk has since passed into modern folklore; how hundreds of little civilian ships braved the mines, dive-bombers and machine-gunners to ferry troops from the beaches to larger naval ships and even, in some cases, all the way back to England several times over. Operation Dynamo brought over 338,000 British, French and Belgian troops back across the Channel. They were put on to trains, and Headcorn station was the first refreshment stop for nearly half of them. Women from all over the district flocked to Headcorn to help out, making sandwiches on an industrial scale in a nearby barn, brewing up tea and washing out the tin cans used as mugs for re-use by soldiers on the next train. Among these ladies were certainly a contingent from High Halden. But the state of crisis was evident even at home, as May Maurice related:

> ... *All the big houses are either hospitals or full of troops, and ambulances from the coast come past me, to avoid the main road I imagine. One stopped at my gate and I saw a nurse (a mere child) get out and go to the leading one and say to the orderly, 'He has gone, poor lad.' Somehow to have gone through all that and Dunkirk and to die before he could see his people. My brother died in an ambulance 25 years ago having fought over the same bit of ground, so sure he was going to prevent this generation doing it.*

The 385th Battery of the 97th (Kent Yeomanry) Field Regiment, who had paraded through High Halden on a recruitment drive only a little over a year before, found themselves stranded in France. Detached to the 51st Highland Division, they fought a fierce rearguard at St-Valery-en-Caux before managing to escape across the Channel on Wednesday 12th June – one of the very few units that made it home after Operation Dynamo had ended.

But the success of the evacuation masked a grimmer reality: that with France conquered, Hitler would now turn his attention to Britain. Everywhere within 20 miles of the Kent coastline was declared a Defence Area, with access only to residents, no outside visitors allowed and military checkpoints to enforce the rules. Sign-posts were painted over and milestones removed or disguised.

On Tuesday 14th May Anthony Eden, the Secretary of State for War, made a radio broadcast appealing for men between the ages of 17 and 65 to join a home defence force which was then being called the Local Defence Volunteers. (Churchill would shortly change its name to the more inspiring Home Guard.) The appeal was an immediate success, with scores of applicants lining up at Tenterden's police station to sign on.

In May 1940 the operational effectiveness of his men was hopeful, to put it mildly. There was no uniform save an 'LDV' armband (which later had to be reissued with the new name). There were no weapons: those with shotguns were asked to bring them on patrol; others were advised to use pikes, pitchforks or kitchen knives taped to broom-handles. For those in reserved occupations, too old for the call-up, or waiting for their call-up, there was much value in the sense that they were doing something in a united spirit towards the defence of the country.

Around fifty men of the parish heeded the call, and many local names, still familiar today, are given on the official muster of High Halden's unit, 'C' Company of the No. 2 Platoon, 2nd (Charing) Kent Battalion: such as Bourne, Buckman, Bugden, Checksfield, Croucher, Hukins, Ledger, Milton, Moore and Tassell. The unit was divided into three squads of ten men each, led by a sergeant and corporal. There were separate teams manning a spigot mortar, Vickers and Browning machine-guns, and a Northover projector – a makeshift anti-tank weapon. Lieutenant A.T. Bassett was the platoon commander, and his sergeant was Alf Buckman.

Basic weapons training with Lee-Enfield rifles (and ten rounds of ammunition) was undertaken in the Memorial Hall, with military personnel formally instructing, and a hundred-yard rifle range was marked out in The Grove for target practice. Further classes in fieldcraft, orienteering and first aid took place in a potting shed behind Halden House. Then on Sunday mornings the men undertook practice out in the field, which usually took the form of a tracking exercise whereby two volunteers would go to ground somewhere in the parish and be sought out by their colleagues.

The invasion scare took hold during June and July. The ringing of church bells was banned on 13th June, with instructions that they would in future only sound to warn of an invasion. The Home Guard were issued with sandbags to set up roadblocks – finding sand in short supply, they used loose soil from fields instead. The bags were transported by the horse and cart of Little Hookstead Farm – loaned by Alf Buckman's relatives – to key locations in the parish: including the main road at Hookstead Green, Wren's Nest Corner, and Woodchurch Road. Farmers were also asked to have wagons and carts ready to be pulled into the roadside for when the emergency signal came.

Given the fact that the density of housing suggested the greatest risk of fire, Tenterden was issued a trailer pump for its fire service by the Home Office, but the scattered outlying villages were not. Instead the Borough was expected to share its appliance when it was not being used to fight fires in Tenterden. Strong representations were made against this, and eventually the Home Office relented, issuing one trailer pump for the Tenterden Rural District – and the site they chose for its base was at High Halden.

Horace Parks, the Tenterden-based Commandant of the District AFS, drew up a comprehensive plan of action regarding the High Halden appliance. 15 men were to be enrolled as firefighters, with George Robinson as Squad Leader. High Halden's local Fire Post would be his garage – the Auto-Service Station at Larasset – where the trailer pump would be stored along with two stirrup pumps, towed to fires by his breakdown lorry, and messages taken on his telephone (High Halden 214). Fires in other villages in the district would be reported to Parks in Tenterden, who would relay the message to High Halden for Robinson's squad to attend. If the fire proved too much for them alone, they would be reinforced by Tenterden Borough's own appliance. A dispatch rider was also to be enrolled to take messages in case the telephone lines were put out of action.

It was a plan born of necessity, but the geography of the area led to some anomalies. For example, High Halden's squad could be sent in the first instance to a fire in the southern part of the district (Rolvenden, Newenden, Wittersham, Stone or Appledore), despite Tenterden's squad being closer. There was no disguising the key fact that resources were desperately thin and difficult priorities would have to be taken in the event of a widespread incident: 'It must be borne in mind that should the High Halden trailer pump be called to another parish, there would be no other appliance left in High Halden to deal with any subsequent fires which may be reported during the absence of the trailer pump.'

The crew got to work with their training, but straightaway it was evident there were problems. Regular drills showed the message relay system from Tenterden to work fine; the problem was summoning all members of the squad from their homes scattered around the parish, as relatively few had their own telephones. Steps were taken to install a fire bell in each member's home, and a quote was obtained at £20 a year – but this was scuppered by red tape from the Ministry of Home Security, who refused to finance it. In the end the Rural District Council put up the money, but much time was lost, and by mid-July the firemen were still not fully trained for their duties.

Out in the Atlantic, the destroyer *HMS Whirlwind* was engaged in hunting U-boats. On board was 35-year-old **Able Seaman George Coleman Bridger**, who had married Doris Blackman seven years earlier and set up home at 15 Hookstead with twin boys Ronald and Alec, both then aged five. On Friday 5th July U-34 got the better of the *Whirlwind*, torpedoing it and causing an explosion that killed 57 men, including Bridger.

The prelude to invasion began on Wednesday 10th July – the official start of the Battle of Britain. For the rest of the month Luftwaffe bombers targeted ports and shipping convoys in the Channel. On Thursday 1st August the order was given to achieve air superiority over the RAF by disrupting the continuing production of aircraft. Tuesday 13th August was designated *Adlertag* – 'Eagle Day' – when the RAF was to be crushed by a knockout blow against all airfields and radar stations. When this failed due to strategic errors from the Luftwaffe, a daily (and nightly) war of attrition followed: a numbers game, with the numbers stacked heavily on the German side. In the first three weeks of July the ARP Control Centre at Tenterden received 142 yellow warnings and 18 red warnings ('action: raiding aircraft expected imminently').

Mass casualties were surely near at hand, and the macabre preparations continued. Each parish now had its own fully fitted-out mortuary. The idea of mass funerals was rejected, but the Clerk of Tenterden Rural District Council – who had undertaken to bear the cost – invited tenders for the performance of simple yet dignified individual ceremonies (with three-quarter-inch plain board coffins, unornamented and unpolished) as cheaply as possible. No tenders came in under the target £5, so the budget was reluctantly raised to £7 10s. Then Horace Ashdown – Tenterden's go-to photographer for family portraits and wedding shots – was put on standby to take pictures of bodies, in cases where identification would be difficult. These steps were all taken secretly by the Council in the belief that, had they become common knowledge, they may have severely damaged morale and even provoked panic.

With anxiety mounting nonetheless, Arthur and Margaret Deacon, of 10 Hookstead Cottages, decided that their children Pamela (four years old) and Peter (four months old) would be better off elsewhere for a while. As Peter remembers:

> *Things were hotting up here, and Dad said we'd better go and stay with our aunt and uncle, who worked for the Duke of Marlborough. So we went, and we were there for the rest of the summer.*

Thus it was that Peter Deacon spent two of his first six months in the opulent surroundings of Blenheim Palace; birthplace of the man of the moment, Winston Churchill, who had become Prime Minister only a few weeks previously.

It is probable that there were soldiers already stationed at Harbourne, as at nearby Tiffenden, but in June and July their presence increased dramatically and they poured in. Two

Bren guns were installed in the tower, one facing south down the driveway and one north towards The Grove and the village. The tower was also used as an observation post, maintaining a round-the-clock watch of the skies for enemy parachutists. When one was sighted a squad of soldiers, always on standby, would drive out to intercept them in a truck with a mounted Bren gun.

Around twenty tents were erected on the lawn to the south of the hall; sleeping quarters for a whole platoon. It was in one of these tents that, on the evening of Friday 19th July, a young officer named Maude was cleaning his revolver. He cocked the gun without realising that one round was still in the chamber. At that moment his fellow officer, 28-year-old **Captain Robin John Wilkinson-Sands** of the Royal Army Service Corps, entered the tent and received the bullet in his chest when the gun went off. He was shot through the heart and died instantly.

All hell broke loose. A medical orderly checked the body and, when it was clear nothing could be done, it was placed on a stretcher and conveyed into the hall. The commanding officer was summoned and H.P. Cole, a soldier of the unit who was on guard duty in Harbourne Lodge at the time, takes up the story:

> *The officer who fired the gun was automatically placed under close arrest, and another Captain from another unit came as prisoner's escort. I was with him all the*

time until his being taken to Aldershot for an enquiry. The OC sent his car for the wife of the dead officer and she arrived at 3.30 the next morning. She lived, I believe, about 70 miles away.

The military court cleared Maude of criminal wrongdoing but he was not permitted to return to his unit. Four days later, on Tuesday 23rd, Captain Wilkinson-Sands was laid to rest at High Halden, with a bearer party from his unit at Harbourne Hall. His is the only military grave from the Second World War in the churchyard, the maintenance of which is still overseen by the Commonwealth War Graves Commission.

There would be no break in the unbearable tension for over a month, and by mid-August the ARP Control Centre had received nearly 50 more red warnings. On Thursday 22nd August Rev. Champion was steeling High Halden's people for the battle to come by reminding them of just who was on the British side:

We cannot question that God's grace has given to our people... gifts of gallantry and devotion, skill and fortitude, wisdom and endurance and unity of mind, without which we could not have withstood the shocks that have come upon us.

A little over a week later several of these shocks came home to High Halden in a big way. The events of Friday 30th August were confused and still confusing, with several frustrating gaps in the surviving documentation, inaccurate statements and hopelessly muddled memories clouding the overall picture. What is apparent is that the skies directly over High Halden saw the heaviest air battle yet, with the loss of perhaps three British fighters that came to earth inside the boundaries of the parish within the space of six hours.

The people were already jittery: two days earlier, the western edge of Tenterden had been bombed in a line stretching from St Michaels to almost Smallhythe — apparently in error, but causing the deaths of a 19-year-old woman and a 13-year-old evacuee boy. Two weeks previously, St Michaels had its railway tunnel bombed and the east window of its church shot in.

At 10.30am radar picked up a mass of enemy aircraft heading across the Channel; their objective was to destroy the major RAF airfields in Kent and Surrey. They were intercepted by 16 RAF squadrons, the first of which, 85 Squadron (Croydon), had been patrolling over Dungeness. Squadron Leader Peter Townshend led a head-on attack of the fifty Heinkel 111 bombers, which were escorted by a protecting ring of Messerschmitts. Pilot Officer John Eglington Marshall's Hurricane was an early casualty of these fighters, sustaining heavy damage in the battle. He managed to guide his aircraft down towards the Weald, but there is confusion as to where he actually made his forced-landing at 11.40am: some sources suggest Langley or Tearnden Farms, just into Smarden; or Green Lane, similarly in Bethersden; or even Tanden Farm, just inside High Halden – though this is likely to be a misreading somewhere along the line. It is a fair assumption that his Hurricane came down close to the north-east boundary of High Halden parish.

In the fourth of five attacking waves that day, at 4.50pm British fighters intercepted enemy bombers at Dover. The convoy scattered and dogfights with their fighter escorts spread out all along the coast. Somewhere over Dungeness, Feldwebel Koch of II/JG26 got the better of 21-year-old **Sergeant John Holt Dickinson** of 253 Squadron (Kirton-in-Lindsey) in his Hurricane. As his aircraft plummeted to earth in a steep dive at 5.15pm, Dickinson managed to bail out and his parachute opened. But nothing further was heard from him; and by 7.45pm he was reported missing. At some point between then and 1pm the following day, he was found dead, still attached to his parachute, and was identified by his personal effects. While no witnesses to what happened could be found, his body was 'riddled with bullets,' and it was generally understood by both the Air Ministry and by his disgusted colleagues in 253 Squadron that he had been callously machine-gunned by enemy fighters while descending by parachute.

Twenty minutes after Dickinson's aircraft was shot out of the sky, 28-year-old **Squadron Leader John Vincent Clarence Badger** of 43 Squadron (Tangmere) came to similar grief in his Hurricane. Badger too bailed out, came down by parachute but was unfortunate enough to land in a tree at Townland Farm, Woodchurch. He was impaled with a branch through the groin, breaking his pelvis and causing terrible internal trauma. Badger was taken to Ashford Hospital but gradually deteriorated; he became seriously ill the following February, and died in June 1941 as a direct result of his injuries.

For years much confusion has surrounded these three incidents, which is not entirely resolved to this day. The only unassailable fact is that while Badger himself landed in Woodchurch, his Hurricane crashed at Plurenden Manor, near Cuckold's Corner, inside High Halden parish. But the official reports of the time assumed this aircraft to be Dickinson's, thanks to the closeness in time between the two crashes. This has since been disproved by a recent excavation of the site, which found material positively identifying the wreckage as Badger's (Hurricane V6548). Dickinson's body is believed to have come to earth near Honeyfield Wood, Bethersden, though his aircraft is officially unaccounted for – an excavation during the 1970s at Tearnden Farm, Smarden, found wreckage but nothing positively identifying it as his Hurricane. These artefacts have been assumed to be from Marshall's aircraft instead, though historians have recently cast doubt on this. Rumours persist of a crash site around the area of Old Chequer Tree Farm, just inside Bethersden, which has yet to be located, but if found may shed light on the circumstances.

Shortly after lunchtime the following day, Saturday 31st August, a large number of Luftwaffe bombers and fighters, heading towards London, were engaged over north Kent. Oberleutnant Hans-Jürgen Ehrig's Messerschmitt was attacked by two Spitfires and a Hurricane, and the engine was damaged. He headed south past Maidstone, where he was chased towards High Halden by Flight Lieutenant Michael Robinson of 601 Squadron (Tangmere), whose guns were empty. He recorded the incident in his logbook:

He [Ehrig] never rose above 100 feet until well south of Maidstone and then throttled back. I overtook him and formated on him, pointing downwards for him to land. He turned away so I carried out a dummy quarter attack, breaking very close to him. After this he landed his Me[sserschmitt] in a field. I threw him a packet of twenty Players and returned to base.

Ehrig had come to ground at the portion of Wagstaff Farm that lay inside the High Halden parish boundary. He had not been able to lower the landing gear but the field was dry, and despite a wing clipping a tree and sending the plane spinning into a field boundary, relatively little damage had been done. Ehrig willingly surrendered to the Home Guard and was then taken away by PC Arthur Day. Meanwhile souvenir-hunters – mostly children – flocked to the spot and liberated several devices from the instrument panel of the cockpit, including the turn and bank indicator, the propeller pitch indicator, and the clock – seen as particularly desirable for its fine German-made Kienzle mechanism.

Four weeks later, Robinson dressed up his account for a propaganda broadcast on the BBC, inventing a story of how he had met the young Luftwaffe pilot ('his English was immaculate; I think he had been to Oxford') while on a skiing holiday in southern Germany early in 1939. As he related it, the pilot had boasted of the Messerschmitt's superiority, and said 'God help you if you ever have to fight us in your old tubs.' Ehrig's Messerschmitt was Robinson's first recorded victory. He would gain or contribute to at least twenty more, rising to the rank of Squadron Leader and receiving both the Distinguished Flying Cross and Distinguished Service Order. He did not return from a patrol in April 1942, and his remains were never found.

Back to 31st August 1940: in the early evening, Flight Lieutenant Forgrave Smith of 72 Squadron, a Canadian pilot known as 'Hiram', came to grief over Romney Marsh:

> *We were attacked by Me 109s at 20,000 feet and turned head on to the attack. I saw puffs of smoke from the cannon of the leading 109 and thought 'missed me' – but not for long: a 20mm cannon shell exploded on hitting the left earphone of my flying helmet.*

A splinter from the shell entered his head by his ear, and exited at the back of his neck, just missing his spine, with further splinters penetrating his left arm. The aircraft was badly damaged and went into a vertical dive. Dazed and barely conscious, Smith opened the hood and tried to bail out, but the speed of his plummeting aircraft was too great, and he was pinned back into the seat by the slipstream.

> *Having gone through the full range of emotions embracing urgency, frustration, consternation, fear, panic and supplication, it was clear to me that owing to the speed at which I was approaching the ground it could only be a matter of moments until I hit it. I then became completely relaxed and resigned myself to imminent extinction.*

In relaxing his muscles Smith was suddenly flung free of the Spitfire and managed to pull his ripcord, descending the last 1,000 feet by parachute. The aircraft crashed in woods near Huntbourne Farm, on the border with Tenterden, and its pilot landed in a nearby field, which he was dragged across by the parachute he was unable to release. Smith then found himself looking down the barrel of a .303 rifle held by a member of the Home Guard, who was suspicious of the airman's exotic accent:

> *I said to him 'British', which explanation he seemed to find less than adequate. I then tried 'English' whereupon he slowly lowered his rifle. By that time it had become clear to him that in my condition, whether friend or foe, I was in no shape to threaten him.*

The fog of war meant that, until relatively recently, the above incident was the subject of some confusion. The Spitfire was identified as a different aircraft, flown by a different pilot who bailed out and received similar injuries on the same day. Newer archaeological evidence, and Smith's own testimony before he died in 1994, now points more conclusively to him having been the pilot who came down at Huntbourne. Smith was flying again three months after his crash. He rose to the rank of Wing Commander, was awarded the Distinguished Flying Cross in 1945, and remained in the RAF until 1957.

At 9.12pm on Tuesday 3rd September, High Halden received its first German bombs – two of them, which are recorded as having fallen somewhere 'near High Halden,' though the exact location was not specified. It is possible that they did not explode on impact. Four days later the Luftwaffe turned their attention to London for the first time; the first day of the Blitz. It was a welcome relief for the RAF who used the change in tactic to put their heavily-bombed airfields back into operation. But this was no comfort to ordinary Londoners, such as Diana Wall, who was by now an active organiser in several spheres, occasionally broadcasting on the BBC, and had transformed her anxieties from the last war into positive action this time around: raising money for Spitfire funds, joining the WVS and running a mobile canteen in Westminster. May Maurice, the neighbour of Diana's mother Susan Jackson, recorded how she lived:

> *The immaculate Mrs Wall, Elizabeth Arden, goes down*
> *every night to a cellar which she shares with a friend*
> *and his wife, their maid, a pair in a double bed, the*
> *caretakers and his wife and two extra casual beds, all*
> *nearly touching.*

Sunday 15th September saw the largest and most widespread air battle of the campaign, involving around 1,500 aircraft which filled the skies and fought until twilight. Facts were not easy to establish in the huge melee, as aircraft seemed to fall out of the sky all over Kent. At least eight Hurricane pilots of 607 Squadron claimed to have damaged a Dornier bomber over Tenterden at 2.45pm.

At 3pm Pilot Officer Denis Crowley-Milling of 262 Squadron was in the thick of it, and managed to get the better of Oberfeldwebel Franz Hessel's Messerschmitt. The aircraft went into a steep dive; Hessel bailed out and his plane slammed into the field directly behind Pope House Farm, just over the High Halden parish border – missing the farm buildings by perhaps fifty yards, and exploding on impact. Hessel, seriously wounded, drifted back across the Tenterden border to land in a field just west of Coever Farm on Swain Road, where he was apprehended by farmworkers and handed over to the authorities for treatment and imprisonment. Crowley-Milling went on to enjoy some hair-raising escapades in the war, flying with Douglas Bader and being shot down over France. With the help of the resistance he escaped to Spain, and returned to Britain via Gibraltar.

But despite all the fighting above, High Halden had so far escaped the major disruption caused by bombing, machine-gunning and crashing aircraft that several other neighbouring towns and villages had experienced. Rev. Champion noted this point in his pastoral letter of Tuesday 24th September:

> *During past months England has been in deadlier peril than at any time throughout its long history. In recent weeks and days it has been subjected to the fury of the long-threatened blitzkrieg... Again today we have reason to marvel at the comparatively little that the enemy has been allowed to accomplish in spite of immense advantages of position and resources.*

The rector would of course have denied it, but this statement was surely tempting fate. Three days later, Friday 27th September, saw the most dangerous and disruptive incident yet.

Feldwebel Herbert Hoffmann had served in the Luftwaffe for three and a half years, and was a veteran of the Battle of France. At noon this day he was flying a Messerschmitt 109 in an operation to clear British fighters from the skies over Kent. Instead a Spitfire got the better of him at 10,000 feet; a bullet grazed Hoffmann's head and he blacked out. He regained consciousness just in time to bail out and watch his aircraft plummet towards the earth over the northern part of High Halden parish. Its descent, at 12.50pm, was witnessed by 12-year-old Gentie Bugden (later Bligh), of Brick House Farm, Further Quarter:

> *This great, dark, camouflaged plane was coming down without the pilot and suddenly turned towards the farmhouse. It nosedived into the road and threw up clay which hit our roof and shattered the rafters.*
>
> *I remember the table was covered in a damask cloth for lunch, and it was covered in dust and debris. Parts of the plane went into the bullock lodge. It was a lucky escape, We were very close.*

Gentie's brother, 16-year-old Richard Bugden, was even closer: out in Pot Kiln Lane, on realising the aircraft was heading directly for him, he dived into the roadside ditch.

May Maurice, down the road at Old House Farm, heard the crash and was one of the first on the scene. She saw the damage to the farmhouse roof and the smashed plane on fire, the flames shooting as high as the house itself. She spotted a woman and baby at the first-floor window just yards away from the smoke and flames – at first she thought they were trapped, but was relieved (and rather astonished) to learn that the mother had taken her child up there to get a better look at the scene.

Hoffmann was captured towards Smarden – Miss Maurice relates that he was 'taken into one of the cottages to have his head scratch bandaged and to have a wash.' While he was being attended to, the authorities set about tidying up the mess he had created. The plane had crashed directly into the road, breaching the main which was now shooting water into the sky. Pot Kiln Lane was closed to traffic, and a steam engine pulled the aircraft engine, cockpit and fuselage out of the clay. The police also turned up to retrieve a machine-gun that Richard Bugden had liberated from the wreckage. However, the salvage operation left the aircraft's propeller deep in the ground, and it was only excavated 53 years later, in October 1993. Even May Maurice took a portion of the windscreen as a souvenir – she later fashioned it into 'an amulet from all perils of the air,' which she sent to her niece whose husband was serving in Africa.

And the Luftwaffe was still not finished with High Halden that Friday. At 9.40pm two high-explosive bombs fell and detonated in a field near the border with Biddenden parish, half a mile north-west of the railway station and just 200 yards from the line itself. High Halden came within a whisker of having both a main road and its rail service put out of action that day. In the event, though, enough patching repairs were made to the road to let vehicles through reasonably quickly; but it took longer to fix the main, and May Maurice recorded in a letter of 10th October that she was still without water two weeks later. She did, however, manage to find a souvenir to use when the service was back on:

> *Yesterday after [dog]fights I picked up a parachute*
> *stirrup (Jerry) which I mean to use for my lavatory*
> *puller, and a Jerry cap with earpieces which will keep*
> *the wind off my ears.*

From a slow start over the summer, High Halden's Battle of
Britain warmed up considerably into the autumn, with
incidents coming thick and fast, and the siren sounding on
most days. Nine-year-old Frank Bourne, who faced a long
walk to school along the road from Durrants Green, was
advised to take a different route:

> *We used to go down as far as one house called Black*
> *House, and then there was a path that led down*
> *through the fields; through the wood at Harbourne...*
> *and we'd come out at the fields to the back of the*
> *school... the footpath up through there, by the shop,*
> *opposite the church... You never knew, if a Jerry saw*
> *us [on the open road] he might just decide to have a*
> *shoot at us.*

Schoolchildren were warned of approaching danger by a
series of whistles, relayed from the siren at Tenterden by
ARP wardens. At the height of the Battle of Britain the
whistles were replaced by a new but rather rudimentary
early-warning-system for the school, which can still be seen
today. It is a piece of steel joist, painted emergency red and
suspended by a hook that is bolted to the wall by the porch
door. When struck with the hammer held on a loop inside,

it resonates with a din loud enough to rouse all the pupils and staff – an anyone in the near vicinity – to take cover. Originally intended to warn of a gas attack, it became the general air-raid warning once it became clear that the more immediate threat was from bombardment.

There was no brick air-raid shelter at the school yet – one had been promised, but demand was so high that it was taking its time in coming. Instead, Miss Rossiter reasoned – along with many others – that the Luftwaffe would never dare to bomb a church. So each time the enemy was overhead and the warning sounded, the pupils were quickly gathered and marched across the road to the ancient church porch, which could just about hold all of them and the staff too. By good timing the timbers had been reinforced by Woodgate's two years previously, and it was thought to be the safest place in an emergency – notwithstanding the several tons of bell-metal hanging above everyone's head.

Each pupil took their notebook and pencil, and classes continued where they had left off. Sometimes the fighting in the skies above raged for hours, and the lessons ran dry, but Miss Rossiter was always ready with more alphabet or number practice – Frank Bourne remembered that she made the children learn their alphabet 'forwards, backwards and sideways.' When even these were exhausted, a crossword was produced and the children encouraged to complete it.

Friday 4th October saw ten high-explosive bombs fall at a point just south of Harbourne Hall, causing a flurry of enormous bangs at 10.15pm but no damage. Eight days later, at 1.15pm on Saturday 12th October, the remnants of an attack that left two women dead in Tenterden saw four bombs from the same load fall in a field south-east of Elmtree Farm. This time two bullocks were killed and one injured.

Ten high-explosive bombs fell in a long one-and-a-half-mile line between Ransley Farm and Grove Farm, off Redbrook Street, at 6.30pm on Friday 15th November – mercifully missing any of the settlements along Plurenden Road and Cuckold's Corner which lay directly below. Then on Wednesday 20th, at 7pm, eleven similar bombs exploded in open fields on the boundary of High Halden and Biddenden, north of Turks Head, Little Bedgebury and Ledger Farms. No damage or casualties were sustained in either incident.

They caused a certain amount of anxiety nonetheless. Such was the frequency of the raids that even the Mothers' Union suspended their meetings – a sure sign of intolerable disruption. There was, however, a way for ordinary people to fight back for the first time: War Weapons Week, held nationwide over 17th-23rd November, encouraged civilians to invest in war bonds and other government securities. In addition, many wished to donate enough to buy a plane (the romantic Spitfire was the most desirable target): High

Halden's Spitfire Fund was overseen by William Woodgate and within a few months had racked up over fifty pounds.

Further support of a practical kind was offered by women's organisations such the Women's Voluntary Service, the Mothers' Union and the Comforts Club, who held regular whist drives at Church Farm to raise money for the materials needed to knit scarves, socks and pullovers for servicemen away from home. These men included several more from the village who were joining up, including the new landlord of the Chequers, Kenneth MacKeleken, who served as an army major and transferred the licence of the pub to his wife Ellen for the duration of his time away from home.

High Halden, along with virtually every other village in Kent by now, had been shaken and battered during the latter half of 1940, and if it had suffered no direct casualties at home, there was enough anxiety, fatigue and stress to have exhausted the people. The prevailing opinion was that reprisals against Germany would be richly deserved, and as the season of goodwill approached, it fell to Rev. Champion to advise his readers against adopting the views of the enemy:

> *Revenge ill befits a Christian man and can achieve no good purpose. 'Be not overcome of evil.'*

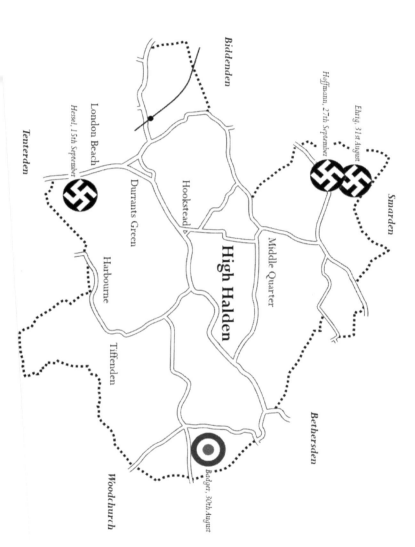

Confirmed aircraft landings and crashes during the Battle of Britain, 1940.

Biddenden

Hoffmann, 27th September

Ebing, 31st August

London Beach

Hessel, 15th September

Tenterden

Smarden

Durrants Green

Hookstead

Middle Quarter

High Halden

Harbourne

Tiffenden

Bethersden

Badger, 30th August

Woodchurch

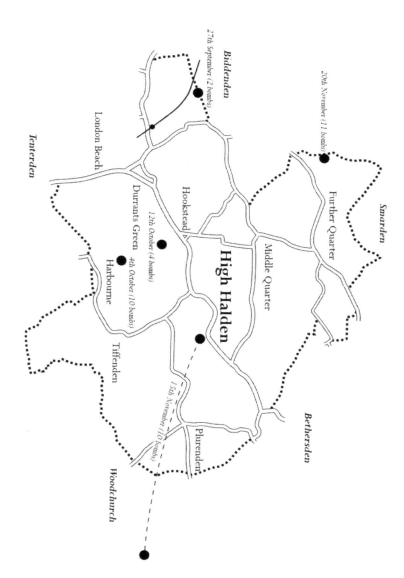

Confirmed bombs during 1940.

27th September (2 bombs)

Biddenden

20th November (11 bombs)

London Beach

Tenterden

Smarden

Hookstead

12th October (4 bombs)

Durrants Green

High Halden

Middle Quarter

Further Quarter

4th October (10 bombs)

Harbourne

Tiffenden

15th November (10 bombs)

Plurenden

Bethersden

Woodchurch

1941

THOSE LIVING IN the south-eastern corner of the parish suffered a great shock on the evening of Sunday 19th January 1941. A 500-lb bomb, dropped by a lone aircraft, exploded on the boundary of two cornfields just west of Kirkbank Cottages, sending a blast wave up Church Hill which shattered the windows of Hillside House. The enormous crater it left is still visible; though slightly diminished by time, weather and soil movement, and its sides covered with dense bracken, it demonstrates how much devastation might have been caused if it had landed in an area of more dense housing. Frank Bourne commented that 'you could have got half a dozen buses in the crater.' And an aerial photograph taken in 1946 clearly shows, five years later, a circular void in the earth surrounded by the tell-tale pattern of blasted soil.

Meanwhile in Tobruk, Libya, 29-year-old **Driver Richard Dance** of the Royal Army Service Corps died on Wednesday 5th February; High Halden's first casualty of the Western Desert campaign. Dance was a builder from a labouring family who had grown up in Goudhurst and Great Chart but moved to Brook Wood on Plurenden Road in 1925, and subsequently to 'Woodend,' Redbrook Street.

The date of his death provokes a mystery, being after the British successfully captured Tobruk from the Italians, but before the German *Afrikacorps* fought back and besieged the city, with British forces trapped inside, for over seven months. It is possible that Driver Dance was injured in earlier fighting and died later of his wounds, or was killed by one of the large number of booby-traps that littered the area and to which drivers were particularly vulnerable.

Back at home, the same month saw a large number of troops billeted in the village centre for the first time. The 56th Battalion Reconnaissance Corps, formed out of the 56th (London) Division that had been in the area for several months, was from January 1941 based at Coursehorn near Cranbrook. On Friday 7th February, the battalion headquarters moved to Halden House, with 'C' Company joining them in and around High Halden – one platoon at Harbourne Hall, one at Brissenden Green (Bethersden) and one at River Hall (Biddenden).

May Maurice had been visited in advance of this to see how many soldiers she could accommodate at Old House Farm:

> *Two nice lads to see about billeting troops on me. I took*
> *them around – 16 in the house they think, and the barn*
> *if needed.*

Then, from Sunday 9th February, she had house-guests for a few nights:

*A very nice French Canadian Colonel who with five
other officers and 150 men and umpteen of the largest
lorries I've ever seen… 6 officers in the house and 150
men in the buildings… They parked their lorries in the
stackyard and when Reveille went at half past one in
the morning for them to move off — pandemonium. Jesus
and his Mother were called in to aid in no uncertain
terms and the night was rent with yells — but they got
out eventually — you never saw such ditches as they left!*

Over the next few weeks soldiers swarmed all over the
parish, taking on reinforcements and conducting tactical
exercises. The 56th Recce Corps' area of operations was in
the shape of a long lozenge lying north of Tenterden,
extending from Biddenden in the west to Ruckinge in the
east, and the Corps had the duty of making armoured patrols
of this Defence Sector each day at dawn. These operations
began on Saturday 1st March, while during the hours of
darkness mobile detachments were placed on standby to be
ready for action at five minutes' notice. Troops from the 1st
Canadian Division are also known to have been conducting
manoeuvres in the High Halden area over Thursday 13th and
Friday 14th March.

On Saturday 15th, the 56th Recce Corps was perhaps
responsible for averting a disaster on High Halden. At 9pm
an enemy aircraft dropped around 50 incendiary bombs in
the vicinity of Brissenden Green, marking a target for high-
explosive bombs to follow. The 'C' Company platoon in the

area quickly extinguished them all, without damage or casualties, and – deprived of their target – the bombers heading westward scattered their payloads aimlessly over Biddenden, Cranbrook and Rolvenden. A couple on a Biddenden farm were killed this night – it is thanks to the soldiers' quick and efficient actions that there was no similar outcome in High Halden.

Agriculture had been heavily disrupted by the events of 1940, particularly the harvest, which had coincided with the height of the air battle. And of course, fit and able young men who might otherwise have helped were being conscripted. To help the farmers and labourers catch up, the clocks did not go back as usual in late October 1940, and were advanced an hour to create Double Summer Time in March 1941. Rev. Champion, who was an early riser, hoped that the scheme would be cancelled to keep the mornings light, but it was not to be.

Good relations grew up between soldiers and civilians in the village and there are very few reports of disciplinary issues from this time. The troops were generally moved from billet to billet after a few weeks, to avoid fatiguing their hosts, but most kept in touch with their old householders and enjoyed cordial dealings. This was especially true of **Serjeant Peter Henry Warner**, a 33-year-old native of Ireland but lately of East Sheen, Surrey, who fell ill with a duodenal ulcer at the end of March and died under anaesthetic at the Benenden Casualty Clearing Station (now Benenden School) on

Tuesday 1ˢᵗ April. During his seven weeks in High Halden he had stayed with at least four households, all of which sent floral tributes to his funeral at Burgess Hill.

The locals recognised that the troops were their guests and needed support, and the Comforts Club set to work raising money on their behalf with a Rummage Sale in the schoolroom – as allowed by Miss Rossiter – which raised the princely sum of £12 3s. They were also richly entertained by the villagers with a series of social evenings in the Memorial Hall – press reports noted that the soldiers responded to these events 'with real warmth and appreciation.'

Some servicemen, however, were not acquitting themselves so honourably. Constantine Voltos, son of the also-named Constantine Voltos of Harbourne Hall, had joined the RAF at the outbreak of war, trained as an air gunner, but had been a thorn in their side ever since. He was arrested and charged more than once for disciplinary offences, and while under guard in early 1941 had managed to escape with an accomplice, George Eagles. The two fugitives made their way to Eagles' home in Birmingham, where Voltos altered the names on two identity cards belonging to the family's daughters – Doris May and Joan Pauline became 'Donald Michael' and 'John Philip' – and with these documents they were able to gain civilian employment as van drivers in Bath. On Saturday 29ᵗʰ March they were arrested after selling two fillets of pork and six kidneys from the van with which they had absconded, and in attempting to get away Voltos nearly ran down a police officer. A week later, Bath magistrates made them pay costs and returned them to their unit for court-martial – which is where the trail goes cold, as the details remain confidential. But it seems likely that, for desertion and theft, both men served at least a year in military detention, from which they could not escape so easily.

Wednesday 16th April saw the heaviest raid of the war so far on London, which suffered eight-and-a-half hours of relentless overnight bombing in which 1,179 people were killed. One of these was **Claud Arthur Stockwell**, aged 63, who grew up at the family home of Bridge Farm, High Halden, before moving to London to become an estate agent at the turn of the century. After several moves, and changes of career, 1941 saw him working as a 'bedding manufacturer' and living at 170 Devonshire Road, Forest Hill with his wife and son. Their house was destroyed and Claud succumbed to his severe injuries in hospital the following day. The house was not rebuilt, and its site is now a nature reserve.

In April an executive order was given stating that, 'owing to the special conditions in the South-Eastern Region,' fire-watching throughout Kent would be subject to compulsory enrolment. All men between 18 and 60 years of age were now compelled to sign up for a watching rota of up to 48 hours per month. There was now not a man in the area who was not doing something for the war effort, and very often these hours were taken as part of Home Guard or ARP duties.

High Halden, though, presented its own challenges in this regard. George Roberts, of 'Falklands,' the overseer of Fire Prevention in the parish, wrote a letter to Tenterden Rural District Council summarising the position:

> *This is a very difficult Parish. There would seem to be very little co-operation in the village. There is at present a private all-night watchman at a builder's yard [Woodgate's], and [the] Warden is in attendance all night at the Head Warden's switch board. Other than that there is no all-night watch kept for incendiaries.*
>
> *I have had a meeting of the Wardens and they have agreed to canvass the area with a view to setting up a point at Wright's Corner where two watchers will be on duty. One will remain at the point and during alerts one will patrol as far as London Beach . . .*
>
> *In conclusion I would point out that in the scattered areas where there are isolated farms and houses it is impossible to set up permanent watches. It has been impressed upon the occupiers of such places that they must be on the alert to deal with their own premises.*

To emphasise his point, Roberts presented a small census of what he found along 500 yards of High Halden's main street:

Eleven houses, in which there are three able-bodied men, of which one is on Home Guard duties, one is in charge of a First Aid Point, one is a farm worker.

There are four permanent invalids, four men between 70 and 80, five women between 70 and 80, and eight other women of varying ages.

At the same time the Ministry of Home Security was coming to a similar conclusion about the fire-fighting arrangements for the district, calling the arrangement with Tenterden Borough 'totally inadequate.' Instead Tenterden Rural District Council was to form its own independent fire brigade, still to be based at High Halden, and with the possibility of erecting dedicated buildings on land adjoining the Auto-Service Station – indeed, the land was requisitioned for this purpose later in the year.

With improvements being made to one emergency service, another was on the agenda. At May's WI meeting (before a practical demonstration of making 'girdle cakes') a discussion was conducted about the lack of a professional nurse in the village. All other surrounding parishes had formed groups in which a local practitioner was responsible for the nursing care within that group. High Halden, it seemed, had been left out of such a group and found itself to be, in Rev. Champion's words, one of 'the very few parishes in England without a nurse.' It was decided that the village should link with its larger neighbour to the south, and within a month the Tenterden and High Halden District Nursing Association had been formed.

Initial progress with the new Association would be slow during its first two years. Much fundraising would be required, at a time when people – having now endured nearly two years of charitable giving – were starting to feel the pinch. Nowhere was this more evident than at St Mary's: the parochial church council signed up to the government's War Risk Scheme, which insured the organ for £100 and church furniture for £200, but charged a premium of £9 each year. This might have been covered by the offerings of the congregation, but attendance was falling off, and Rev. Champion complained rather bitterly about those 'to whom it might seem to matter little or nothing at all if all our beautiful old churches were bombed to pieces tomorrow.'

Perhaps it wasn't so much indolence, or apathy, but the heavy demands from other aspects of life. The trailer pump crew saw a number of resignations this spring, and the 56th Recce Corps reported that their work in helping to train local Home Guard units was being hampered by the fact that many members had agricultural duties. It was also an unwelcome surprise to discover that the tiny government grant was not sufficient to set up a First Aid Point in the parish, and that the villagers needed to equip themselves for the purpose. A subscription list was opened for this, too, but the whole situation did nothing to ease the anxiety people still felt for their own safety. The 56th Recce Corps left

Halden House for Uckfield on 19ᵗʰ May, so for the time being there was little reassuring military presence in the village, either.

Tenterden Rural District Council's rate book for 1941-42 still exists, giving us a useful picture of the few local properties that remained in military occupation once Halden House was returned to its owner, Commander Ford. The Memorial Hall was still exclusively for military and Home Guard use, though this did occasionally extend to civil defence personnel, such as for ARP and fire service lectures. Harbourne Hall – the mansion, grounds and premises – were still occupied, as was 1 Harbourne Cottages. 1 and 2 Hales Place Cottages completed the list: as these were all now regarded as Crown Property for the time being, they would be allowed a reduced contribution to the council rates. Though not mentioned on this list, Hathewolden Grange is also understood to have been in military hands at some point during the middle years of the war.

The Ministry of Agriculture and Fisheries introduced a War Agricultural Executive Committee to each county. The 'Kent War Ag' was tasked with improving the efficiency of every farm in terms of its management and production, with a key emphasis on ploughing up pasture land to be sowed with arable crops that would stretch further. To this end, 1941 saw the beginning of the National Farm Survey, a nationwide exercise to assess the efficiency of each farm, which was to take over two years to complete. After an initial census on 4th June, the bulk of High Halden's assessment (the Primary Farm Survey) came in the autumn, when each farmer received a visit from Horace Willsher of Moat Farm, who filled in the bare facts of the farm (its tenure, condition, and that nature of its water and electricity supply). Then a few months later, a county inspector came to check that Willsher's survey was correct, and to speak to the farmer about what had already been done and what was being planned. This gave rise to the most controversial part of the assessment: the management of each farm was graded A (well), B (fairly well) or C (badly). If a score of B or C was down to old age or lack of capital it was recorded as such, and if it came down to the personal failings of the farmer, the reasons why would be recorded.

Around half of High Halden's farms received an A grade. The remainder fell short for a wide variety of reasons, not all of which were necessarily the fault of the farmer. Several were trapped in a vicious cycle, lacking the capital to improve their productivity, or had found that the circumstances of the war had reduced the market for their produce. Several farmers were noted as suffering from ill-heath ('very deaf, suffers from a rupture, [but] is doing his best'); some had started farming as a pastime ('an invalid for some years and has taken this up as a health-making hobby'); others simply lacked the time to devote to their farms wholeheartedly.

Old age was a perennial issue, giving rise either to incapability or outdated methods. A lady in her eighties was recorded as 'not capable of looking after this holding... which has been badly neglected and is in a very poor state.' In a couple of cases the husband was largely incapable of the work, most of which fell to the wife instead. Others sublet to other farmers and thus had little control over how their own land was used.

There were occasional instances of laziness, bloody-mindedness or 'limited capacity for management.' One farmer, described as 'old and obstinate,' admitted that he 'does not like arable farming' and was listed for a further government inspection. Farms were also marked down for being untidy or disordered ('everything very dilapidated and rough'). Some were simply beyond help. One gave the impression 'that he would lose his crop for want of suitable manure and management... I was not favourably impressed.' Another gave no sense of 'having any knowledge of farming.' Others were baldly described as a 'very poor farmer' or 'not a farmer.'

It was clear that farmers needed as much help as could be given, and thus was born the Women's Land Army which, until conscription was introduced for women in December, was a voluntary organisation for those wishing to help. Popular jobs were attending to livestock, particularly horses, and milking cattle. After an initial cool reception, the Land Girls not only proved themselves invaluable but, in most cases, at least the equal of their male co-workers. One such example was Miss D.M. Swaffield, who arrived at Tiffenden Manor in the autumn of 1940 and had already completed six months' service by the time most others were joining up. Also at this time, and in preparation for the harvest to come, the Kent War Ag started building a hostel for the seasonal agricultural workers who would need billeting over the summer.

Germany's unexpected invasion of Soviet Russia in June led many to breathe a sigh of relief: by opening a new front in the East, Hitler turned his attention away from Britain – for the time being, at least. But this welcome news did nothing to lessen the anguish of those with relatives serving in the armed forces, and facing peril both at home and abroad.

Sapper Reginald ('Reggie') Biggs, a native of London, had been in the care of Sydney and Edith Rootes of 1 Hillfield Villas since 1923, and formally adopted by them a little later. At the outbreak of war he was working as a gardener in Cranbrook, but soon joined the 501st Field Company of the Royal Engineers. On Friday 18th July he was killed accidentally, aged 24, while training with high explosives at Shorncliffe Barracks, near Hythe. Rev. Champion wrote that 'he died on active service as truly as if he had fallen on the field of battle.' It was not the first wartime tragedy for the family: almost exactly 25 years previously, Sydney's younger brother Clement Rootes had died while in Turkish captivity in what is now Iraq.

In spite of all the preparations and support given to agriculture, the summer of 1941 was blighted by bad weather and a disappointing harvest was achieved. Nonetheless the church's Harvest Thanksgiving takings were £10 12s 1d, a sum that was divided equally between the Royal Agriculture Benevolent Institution and the RAF Benevolent Fund. Bolstering this were the efforts of the Comforts Club, who held another Whist Drive at Church Farm in November – two months previously, they had sent 48lbs of knitted comforts to the RAF. Also in November came the welcome (and unique) news that the Kent County Spitfire Fund, to which High Halden had been paying in for over a year, had raised the target £100,000. Kent was therefore to be the first county to have a Spitfire squadron named after it.

It must have proved a strange irony, then, that High Halden had seen no enemy action in 1941 since January's solitary bomb blast. Despite the quiet, the ARP and Rescue Party (both under the command of William Woodgate) continued their activities. The wardens, particularly those who had recently joined, attended a series of four lectures at the Memorial Hall by a local instructor. The Rescue Party, despite a shortage of vehicles, undertook a training course and spent a Sunday working with the Swanley Mobile Reserve on the outskirts of London – an area which had seen plenty of devastation.

A 1930s aerial view of High Halden from the south-east.

Right: A pre-war scene in the Chequers. (l-r) George Button, George Woodgate, 'Dumpling' Ledger and Sam Adams.

Below: Charles Welsh Mason, adventurer and hermit, at his self-built home in Brook Wood.

The school's air-raid alarm, still present on the original school porch.

Right: the grave of Robin Wilkinson-Sands in High Halden's churchyard.

Below: Harbourne Hall, where his death occurred.

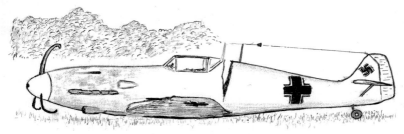

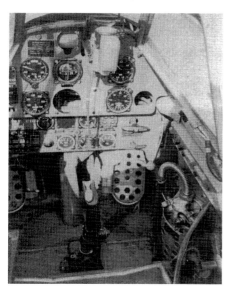

Top: the Messerschmitt flown by Hans-Jürgen Ehrig that force-landed at Wagstaff Farm, 31st August 1940.

Above: a sketch of the scene as remembered by Howard Millen.

Left: the cockpit of the aircraft. Souvenir hunters had already taken several instruments from the panel.

The spot of Herbert Hoffmann's Messerschmitt crash by Brick House Farm.

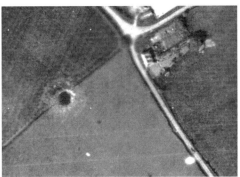

Left: a 1946 aerial photograph of the crater produced at Kirkbank Corner by a bomb on 19th January 1941.

Below: the crater today.

The plans for RAF High Halden, 1942.

An aerial photograph of USAAF High Halden from May 1944.

Today's view, looking north at the point where the main runway crossed Pot Kiln Lane. Note the flat landscape and the absence of ditches and mature hedges.

Gates Farm, occupied by officers as the airfield headquarters.

358th Fighter Group ground personnel start the engine of P-47 Thunderbolt 'Chunky' at USAAF High Halden.

Crew chiefs of the 365th Fighter Squadron at USAAF High Halden.

Harris Wood, where the Americans buried their food on leaving High Halden.

An aerial photograph of the site of USAAF High Halden from May 1946, showing the scars the runways left on the landscape.

Right: Peter Deacon's victory statement, issued to all schoolchildren in 1946.

Below: the panel later added to High Halden's war memorial, marking those lost in the Second World War.

1939 – 1945

R. BIGGS	1941	P.L.FANNING	1944
G.C. BRIDGER	1940	C.J. HOGBIN	1945
W.J.C. CAMBRIDGE	1944	L.E.G.WALL	1944
R. DANCE	1940	D.E. WARD	1942
P.C. ETTRIDGE	1944	J.E.R. WRIGHT	1943
R. J. WILKINSON-SANDS	1940		

On Friday 10th October a notice had appeared in the *Kentish Express*:

> *Notice is hereby given that it is proposed to remove the railings surrounding the graves and vaults in the churchyard of St Mary's High Halden, unless objection is raised by anyone interested within 14 days.*

Despite the sadness some may have felt, there were no such objections, knowing that this metal would serve a nobler purpose as ships, planes and armaments. Rev. Champion was remarkably sanguine about the proposal, believing it would both help the war effort and improve the churchyard:

> *The difficulty of keeping this tidy and in good order is great, and the rusty railings, which form a harbourage for brambles, young trees and rubbish, add to the problem. They will be better away.*

And in outlining changes to the times of the festive services, in order to comply with the blackout, the rector added:

> *A strange Christmas it must needs be, with the nations which have professed and called themselves Christians at war to the death!*

1942

AT THE START of the year the residents of Further Quarter lobbied William Woodgate, as Head Warden, to push for a telephone kiosk to be installed there. This, it was argued, was essential for efficient communication to and from that remote district, and would be of principal use to the ARP services. Tenterden Rural District Council put the proposal to the General Post Office – who until 1969 were responsible for the provision of telephones – and a kiosk was duly installed by Poorsfield a few months later.

Other improvements attempted to plug gaps in the civil defence services. William Woodgate got hold of a three-ton Bedford lorry which, once drop sides and tilt loops had been fitted, and the tyres retreaded, was given over to the Rescue Party. Woodgate's business was finding itself more in demand than ever with wartime contracts, and his many and varied duties were proving too much to take on. He began to share the Rescue Party duties with Mr Musgrave, and while Woodgate remained Head Warden for the time being, he felt unable to take on the position of Head Fire Guard as well. Captain Fitz-Jenyns was approached but he was already acting as Salvage Warden. Consequently the position took several months to fill.

An embarrassing episode occurred in March when George Roberts, who had also resigned as Fire Prevention overseer a few months previously, fell foul of the Ashford police in a licensing matter. The precise details are not known, but there was some disagreement between Roberts and the local ARP Sub-Controller, Colonel Francis Cosens of Tenterden, as to Roberts' car being registered for ARP duties. Cosens believed that it was not; Roberts countered that it was, and complained that the Ashford police 'had been given a false impression as a result of the Sub-Controller's statement.' Cosens outlined the full facts to the police and the matter was not pursued, but it was an unhelpful indication of how far red tape had extended into everyday life. Cosens was a regular visitor to High Halden in these times, conducting training courses for the wardens in the Memorial Hall.

Concerns were now being raised that agricultural labourers in the fields, who were most in need of cheap, nourishing meals, were going without, and that this was affecting their productivity. For these men and women the journey to a source of hot food in the middle of the day was too time-consuming to bother with, and they generally made do with a limp sandwich. This spring the Ministry of Food came up with the solution: a Rural Pie Scheme, administered locally, by which hot meat pies would be made and delivered daily to those working away from their homes or the village centres. Initially it was suggested that the baker would distribute the pies as part of his usual bread round, but it became evident that the scheme would soon outgrow this arrangement. The Women's Voluntary Service for the Tenterden Rural District leapt on the task, and drew up plans for its own members to deliver the pies.

Orders were taken on Saturdays and Wednesdays, and Mondays and Thursdays used for sourcing ingredients and preparing the pies. Then on Tuesdays and Fridays they were baked, and the WVS ladies used a network of bicycles to deliver them direct to the fields in the outlying parts of the district. Despite being a bigger undertaking than that of Tenterden town's own scheme, and covering a much larger area, the Tenterden Rural operation was up and running by May, whereas Tenterden's own had to wait another year. By July the district's bakers were churning out over 8,000 pies a week – although there were teething problems when some pies were found to contain less than the requisite 1d's worth of meat. Once these bakers had received a stern letter the situation improved, and the scheme was such a success that it continued throughout the war.

Things may have been quiet at home, but there were occasional reminders of the threat that flew above, and the old 'gas scare' had not yet been discredited. In May each parish was issued with a bin in which to place any clothing that had been exposed to gas in an attack. The bins would then be collected and transported to Tenterden for decontamination. It was an act of caution that would thankfully never be put into practice. The only garments worthy of comment at this time were those of Rev. Champion, who had been gifted a new set of vestments that he wore for the first time at Easter. Some found them uncomfortably reminiscent of Roman Catholicism; others just found them plain risible, but the rector brushed off the snide remarks: 'We need not grudge them their little amusement, nor take their criticisms too seriously.'

The district Rescue Party sharpened up the skills and responses of its members with a number of training activities this spring. Together with the parish First Aiders, they carried out a 'very satisfactory' practice in the ruins of St Michaels Grange, which had been extensively bomb-damaged with the loss of two lives in October 1940. William Woodgate asked the district ARP Committee whether arrangements might be made for the squad to hold friendly competitions against other Rescue Parties in the neighbourhood; and while the New Romney team were not willing, a competition was held against Ashford late in the year. (Sadly, the outcome was not recorded.) Woodgate was also given special permission to construct a shelter in his yard to keep the rain off the all-important rescue vehicle.

Then, around June, life began to get busier, particularly in the northern part of the parish. In planning for the invasion of Europe, the Air Ministry were scouting locations all over Kent to assess where might be suitable for temporary airfields. Exercises were conducted along the country lanes to test access and work out how well the neighbourhoods could cope with the increased traffic and troop movements. May Maurice noted that for a few weeks the roads were filled with

> ... *streams of every kind of khaki vehicle and troops marching and buzzing DRs [dispatch riders] on motor bikes up and down the road day and night, mostly night. Incessant knocks at the door, cups of tea, eggs, bread etc, to sustain the combatants. They are very grateful and full of talk and I enjoy it all – but the noise!*

By early July things had calmed down again, and Miss Maurice described how 'people have taken to grazing the road sides, there is so little risk of cars!' The reason was that, with all assessments completed, High Halden had been shortlisted as a location for one of Kent's eight Advanced Landing Grounds.

The site chosen was at the northeast extremity of Further Quarter, on land between Pot Kiln Lane and Bethersden Road. The plans allowed for two runways: the main one, 4,440 feet long, aligned north-east to south-west; and a secondary one, 3,840 feet long and running west to east – with the two intersecting to form a flattened V-shape. Access to the airfield would be at the corner of Pot Kiln Lane by Brick House Farm – close to the site of the Messerschmitt crash in September 1940 – and through the drive to Gates Farm which – ideally set well back from the road for security purposes – would be taken over as the officers' headquarters.

Land would need to be requisitioned from Wagstaff Farm (based in Biddenden but with much land in High Halden), Brick House Farm, Pear Tree Farm, Dents Farm, Haffenden, Gates Farm and Old House Farms. There followed several anxious weeks as the authorities decided just how much rent could be paid to the owners, and whether the occupiers could stay in their homes. Miss Maurice, in the last-named of these, was eventually allowed to keep her house, farm buildings and 16 acres of land running along the road:

> *They are taking the heart out of the farm and have been*
> *meanly cheese-paring beyond belief, but at least I'm not*
> *a refugee… A meagre rent and nothing to compensate*
> *for the lack of one's livelihood.*

The authorities reminded her constantly that if she remained at Old House Farm, she would do so under sufferance and at her own risk. They would not be taking responsibility for loss of property, life or limb occasioned from, for example, the use of live ammunition in the fields behind her house, or an air crash.

Had she but known it, the inherent perils of flying were being made apparent some 250 miles away on Saturday 22nd August, when a Beaufighter aircraft with two occupants was attempting to make a landing at Catfoss airfield, in the East

Riding of Yorkshire. There are conflicting accounts of what happened to it, but the most likely is this: that the aircraft bounced off the runway, damaging the landing gear; the pilot aborted the attempt and gunned the engines, choking them and causing a failure; and the plane crashed at nearby Brandesburton to the west. The aircraft caught fire: both men were pulled clear of the wreckage; the pilot survived but the observer died of his injuries. He was 21-year-old **Aircraftman Constantine Phillip Voltos**, the wayward son of Constantine Voltos, erstwhile of Harbourne Hall but lately of Kensington. His son's death is the last piece of evidence to link the Voltos family to High Halden. It seems that the father's creditors caught up with him, as council rate books henceforward show the owner of Harbourne to be a bank, suggesting its foreclosure against debts. But however history records their circumstances, and past behaviours, the death of this young serviceman was a tragic end to a short and errant life.

In chasing non-payment of rates, Tenterden Rural District Council was more lenient towards those who clearly had no means to do so, such as Charles Mason whose poverty was only too clear. He was summoned in September but his circumstances caused his arrears to be written off. It is evident that, by the autumn of 1942, most households were similarly struggling.

With continued disruption to shipping, and the two disappointing harvests of 1940 and 1941, rations were being reduced more and more. Queues were everywhere, particularly in the nearby towns of Tenterden and Ashford. Blackouts were tiresome and enforced by officials viewed to be inflexible, stirring up resentment. There was still no sign of the Americans, who had entered the war in December 1941 and were slowly making their way across the Atlantic.

Fewer people were attending church, especially in bad weather, and even fewer seemed willing to put their hands into their pockets to keep the place going. Rev. Champion did not point the finger, but instead saw that the wider circumstances of the war were to blame:

> *Before the war there were not a few who were ready to give willingly of their substance; but now we are reminded that 'Five pounds is five pounds.'*

A tin-crushing machine was loaned to Tenterden Rural District for one week only, and it made its way around the area, stopping in each parish for a few hours. While Captain Fitz-Jenyns' efforts as Salvage Warden had succeeded in accumulating a huge pile of material by Lion Farm, it was not collected and began to stink, causing a public nuisance. In such circumstances the mantra of 'waste not, want not' began to grow thin.

Work was proceeding on the new airfield, with RAF engineers levelling the ground by filling in ditches and removing trees. The runways and taxi lanes were made of Sommerfield Tracking, a system of steel mesh panels pinned to the ground with angled steel bars, and a new drainage system was installed to keep water off them. Four hangars were built to house the aircraft, as well as administration huts. Miss Maurice was particularly saddened by the changes:

> *Our oak trees in their flaming glory, flaming chequer trees felled, hedges grubbed and the fields turned into a khaki mass of mud. What waste, what devastation. We swarm with blue and grey uniforms. I (so far) hold on to my house, buildings and 16 acres. If I have to go they say that they will try and give me a week's notice if they can.*

Of all the farmers affected by the work, at least one – William McLeod of Dents and Pear Tree Farms – decided to sell all his livestock, which happened at an auction held on Thursday 1st October.

On the same day, out in the East China Sea, the *Lisbon Maru*, a Japanese troopship containing British and Canadian prisoners of war captured in the fall of Hong Kong, was taking its human cargo back to Japan when it was mistakenly torpedoed by an American submarine. The prisoners were locked in the hold by their captives; those who managed to escape were machine-gunned in the water. Among the few who avoided both drowning and being shot was **Warrant Officer John Edmund Jupp**, aged 40, of the Hong Kong Volunteer Naval Reserve. A strong swimmer, he made it to land and was looked after by Chinese villagers but was recaptured by the Japanese a few days later. He endured a terrible journey to Japan, with sick men dying all around him. Jupp himself fell ill and died on Monday 12th October at Kobe. His wife Faith, and their two young daughters, had managed to escape Hong Kong via Australia and were living in High Halden at the time of his death.

The Western Desert Campaign was about to reach its climax with the start of the Second Battle of El Alamein on Friday 23rd October. Four days into this great push, on Tuesday 27th October, fell **Major Denis Erskine Ward**, aged 30. Born in Guildford, and the grandson of Sir William Erskine Ward, a celebrated Civil Service officer in India, Denis was a career soldier and member of the Royal Tank Regiment of the Royal Armoured Corps before the war. He had married his wife Kathleen (known as Susan) only six months earlier, and settled at 'Parkhurst' in High Halden. Nothing was heard from him after El Alamein and his death was not confirmed until June the following year. After the war his widow, who had divorced in order to marry Ward, was reconciled with her first husband and remarried him.

Whatever the human cost of the victory, it was a victory nonetheless, and as Churchill put it a couple of weeks later, 'This is not the end. It is not even the beginning of the end. But it is, perhaps, the end of the beginning.' For the first time in nearly thirty months the church bells were allowed

to ring in celebration on Sunday 15th November, as Rev.
Champion recounted:

> *The Battle of Egypt was a real victory, and it was*
> *outstanding and it was the first positive success on a large*
> *scale which has come our way — a real gleam in the*
> *darkness... We have gone through difficult days together,*
> *and shall have, it may be, many more to go through; but*
> *no-one can fail to experience a lift of the spirit, as when*
> *sunshine peeps through the clouds on a rainy day.*

Shortly afterwards came the final reckoning for much of the
village's hard work over the year. The Comforts Club had
sent off 769 garments in 1942; from 545 in 1940 and 608 in
1941, and with hope for the further increase in 1943. These
items found their way to the those stationed in India, the
Royal Corps of Signals, and the Merchant Navy. The Pie
Scheme reached its peak in the first spell of winter,
producing pies at the rate of nearly 10,000 every week,
ensuring that those working in the fields were well-fed. And
then the final accolade: Warships Week, with a target of
providing the cost of two motor launches, had actually
managed to supply four.

But at Christmas 1942 the most obvious cause for optimism
in High Halden was that fact that there had been not a hint
of enemy action within the parish since January 1941, nearly
two years previously. Alongside all the other good news, to
many it seemed that final victory could be closer than ever.

1943

AT 4.36AM ON Monday 18th January an enemy bomber was observed at Biddenden, heading north towards Headcorn. It dropped a cluster of incendiaries which landed at Appleton Farm, Frittenden, and quite possibly also a parachute mine which failed to explode. A later investigation records that the farmer saw the parachute sticking out of the ground and, assuming that a dead airman was half-buried in the impact hole, tried to pull him out: 'What he said on discovering his mistake is not recorded.' The aircraft was spotted by the Headcorn observer post circling three times, perhaps to confirm any damage caused. If so, the crew were to be disappointed, and in any case the incendiaries had been wasted, as there was no viable target of any kind in the area.

Investigators found it impossible to say just how many enemy bombers were present over the next three-quarters of an hour, but cross-referencing with the logs made by various observer posts suggests at least two, possibly three. They were either lost, woefully inaccurate in their aim, or misinformed about targets on the ground. They were also under great pressure from defending British aircraft who were recorded as being very active during this raid. The result was the first enemy activity over High Halden for two years, nearly to the day, and a night of terror that would long be remembered.

At around 5am another plane came in from the east, which bombed the Wye area, missed the significant target of Ashford completely, and dropped further bombs in woodland in the Wissenden area of Bethersden parish. A few minutes later, at 5.06am, another aircraft was spotted north of Cranbrook, heading west but making a sharp about-turn north of Goudhurst, though it does not appear to have targeted anything.

Either one of these three aircraft could have been the one observed at 5.14am north of Sissinghurst, heading east in a line roughly parallel to what is now the A262. At Biddenden it took a wide arc to the south over Stede Quarter and at 5.17am it was directly over Durrants Green, High Halden, when it released thirteen bombs.

Twelve of these were of the standard high-explosive *Sprengbombe Cylindrisch* type known as the SC-50. But the first in the load was a *Abwurfbehälter* (AB-500) cluster bomb, a steel canister full of incendiaries. It landed in the front garden of Orchard House, home of the Misses Richford, and scattered the firebombs – depending on the exact type, it could have held either 28 or 37 – over a distance of forty yards, all over the main road and the land between Blackborne Cottage and Homestall Farm. Luckily, there was nothing there to catch fire and the bombs burned themselves out without damage.

The first high-explosive bomb landed close by, only five yards from Orchard House itself, blowing in the front windows and leaving a crater in the drive.

The second and third SC-50s fell at Homestall Farm. Neither detonated; instead they left eighteen-inch entry holes in the earth, one burrowing its way diagonally under the farmhouse – these would not be discovered for a little while yet. Bomb four fell at Moat Farm on the north side of the road, and managed to explode forming no crater and causing no damage.

Durrants Court, the home of the Hon. Eveline Godley, received the next four bombs. Of these, the first could have been much worse: it exploded just five yards from the house, but some way beneath the surface, causing an underground cavern known as a *camouflet*. Were it not for the heavy Wealden clay that contained the blast, this could have been far more dangerous to the adjacent building than a direct hit. The next bomb landed ten yards from the house but did not explode; the third produced no crater but caused some damage to the house, starting a small fire. The fourth landed in the orchard to the rear.

Bombs nine and ten landed in the rear garden of St Anne's, home of Thomas and Alice Biddles. The first bomb set fire to a tool shed; the second did not explode. Unfortunately for Mr Biddles, the tool shed contained his supply of cider, and he was most annoyed to lose the lot.

The last two bombs fell in a field by the junction of the Biddenden Road and Oak Grove Lane, south of the Old Thatched Barn (now Moat Barn) and north of Apple Tree Cottage. The first caused another camouflet; the second, a crater fourteen feet across and four feet deep.

The inhabitants of Durrants Green stumbled from their homes in the early winter dawn and rushed to help those caught in the blasts, shortly followed by the Air Raid Wardens, First Aid crew and as many members of the Trailer Pump squad as could be mustered. To their immense relief, all civilians were accounted for, nobody was even slightly injured, and the small fires had been brought under control. But as dawn broke and light returned it became clear that unexploded bombs lay underground, and throughout the morning the area was evacuated pending the arrival of a bomb disposal unit.

One who did not receive this message was Dickie Waterman, owner of Homestall Farm, who was on Home Guard night duty elsewhere in the parish. He ended his shift that morning, somehow evading all the activity in the area, came home and went to bed, thinking nothing of the sizeable hole in the ground by his back door. He was rudely awoken a few hours after with the news that a bomb lay directly under his house that could go off at any time.

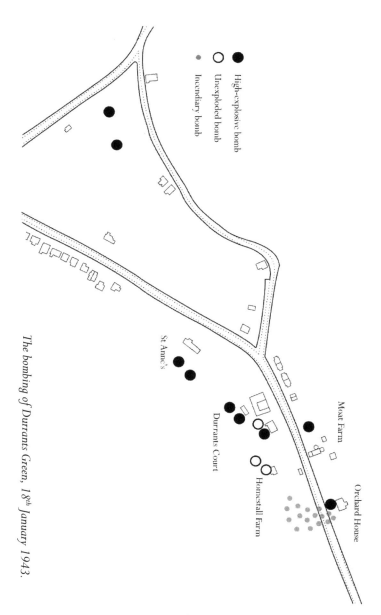

Legend:
- ● High-explosive bomb
- ○ Unexploded bomb
- • Incendiary bomb

St Anne's

Durrants Court

Homestall Farm

Moat Farm

Orchard House

The bombing of Durrants Green, 18th January 1943.

Once the military were involved, events moved quickly. The road was closed entirely to motor vehicles between Durrants Green and Hookstead, with a diversion set up in a long loop to the north: starting at the Man of Kent, past Crampton House, Wren's Nest, and emerging at Hookstead Green. This narrow route became clogged with traffic, particularly buses, with passing vehicles churning up the winter mud along the verges.

Seven houses nearest to the unexploded bombs were evacuated, and their inhabitants billeted elsewhere in the parish. Of the four viable devices, three – at Homestall Farm, Durrants Court and St Anne's were dealt with quickly. But the fourth – underneath Homestall farmhouse itself – took far longer to make safe and then retrieve, and Rev. Champion wrote nine days later that 'it seems probable the house will have to be demolished in order to dig it out.' This did not happen, and it is testament to the skill and ingenuity of the bomb squad that this historic old building was saved.

The process for making safe an unexploded bomb during the war differed from today, where technology has advanced such that a contained explosion at the point of impact is considered the safest approach. Clearly, in the case of Homestall Farm, this was not appropriate. Instead, once the bomb had been accessed, it was manually defused by separating the detonator from the explosive within. The device was then brought to the surface and transported to a 'bomb cemetery' where the volatile material could be safely disposed of. High Halden parish was fortunate – though that was perhaps a matter of opinion – to host one of two such bomb cemeteries in the Tenterden Rural District, at the south side of Trottingale Wood, between Tiffenden Manor and Little Tiffenden Farm. A 1946 aerial photograph shows a patch of ground pock-marked with the scars of various controlled explosions – the legacy of UXBs found all over the district.

A few days after the blast, investigators from the Research and Experiments Department of the Ministry of Home Security visited the site to compile a report on the raid. These men, recruited from the Flying Squad and with wide investigative experience, were tasked with looking into all the circumstances, and it is from their report – classified as MOST SECRET until 1972 – that much of the foregoing information is gleaned. They found that all of the bomb craters, with the exception of that in Durrants Court orchard and the last in an open field, had since been filled in. Nonetheless, they were able to identify the bombs as SC-50s from a combination of their craters and the damage caused. At the sites at Moat Farm and Durrants Court, where two bombs formed no craters at all, traces of magnesium suggested that these were variants with an incendiary element, designed to burst into flame upon impact, rather than explode – the fact that a small fire was caused at Durrants Court seems to bear this out.

This was the most destructive and disruptive occurrence on High Halden so far. Rev. Champion devoted the entirety of his address in February's parish magazine to it, which found him in philosophical mood:

To those who had suffered loss and damage, as well as to our other parishioners who have experienced distress and inconvenience in the ill-fortune of war, we express our deep sympathy. At the same time our predominant feeling must be one of profound thankfulness that this visitation was accompanied by no loss of life or limb, and considerably less damage than might have been expected...

This incident awakens many reflections... Chance? Well, the odds were enormously against these bombs falling just where they did, instead of somewhere amid the acres and acres of surrounding woodland and open fields. On the other hand, once the bombs fell where they did, the odds seem to be that they might have done vastly more harm than they did... That is all we can say. Not very satisfactory perhaps? And certainly nothing to be thankful about, for there is no-one to be thankful to! Relief, yes; but thankfulness? No.

But Providence? Our heavenly Father? If we believe in the living God — who controls all the vicissitudes of circumstance — is there any place left for chance?... I think not. And for all God's gift of free determination

> *to man, we must not suppose He allows himself to be*
> *shouldered out of the picture. He remains in sovereign*
> *control. He caters for the sparrow. He numbers the hairs*
> *of our head. He ordains its billet for every 'chance'*
> *bullet, and for every bomb released at a venture...*
> *Therefore it is God our Father whom we must thank,*
> *alike for our deliverances, our warnings and all the*
> *discipline of our lives... It is He — and not chance —*
> *who determines the manner and moment of our passing,*
> *and calls us to our account.*

At the end of 1942 William Beveridge, the Chairman of the Social Insurance Committee, had published a detailed report proposing widespread societal reform to slay the 'five giants of Want, Disease, Ignorance, Squalor and Idleness.' The National Insurance scheme would be expanded, allowing the benefits system to be reformed, and the introduction of free healthcare for all at the point of supply. This report would be the blueprint to the post-war Welfare State, and it was widely supported by a public desperate for some good to come out of the war. But not by politicians, who regarded it as well-meaning but idealist (Conservatives) or liable to upset the unions (Labour). Churchill himself was dismissive, believing it would cause economic harm to a Britain likely to be in huge debt after the war.

But social reform was very much on the agenda in early 1943, and foremost among this was the question of church schools, of which High Halden boasted a fine example. It was suggested that voluntary church schools – that is, funded by public subscription and supported by the Church – had had their day, and that they should have their religious status removed and taken out of Church control. There were two alternatives: one was to allow state-sponsored 'undenominational' teaching; two, a form of 'moral' teaching without religion. Champion's reaction to both of these options was harsh and unyielding:

> *The former has been tried and found wanting… The latter is simple paganism, and would result in the dominance of a totalitarian state such as we see in Nazi Germany.*

Not everyone in the parish appreciated the importance of school as much as their rector, and school attendance cases brought before the Cranbrook magistrates reached their peak at this time. Parents were generally fined £1 each time they were found guilty of having failed to ensure their children went to school. Several High Halden families were repeat offenders, and a particularly severe case would be heard later in the year. That said, many would claim that an outbreak of measles – 28 cases – at the school early in 1943 had compelled them to keep their children away.

Rev. Champion clearly also feared that ending religious education would lead ultimately to moral failings, instances of which he was observing in High Halden. At his instigation, Mrs Batchelder became the parish representative of the newly-rejuvenated district Moral Welfare Association. This had been in abeyance for some years – and it showed, as the Rector was not shy to point out:

> *It appears to be the case that we have not escaped the deterioration which war tends to cause in national character. Standards have slipped especially as regards respect for property and as regards questions of sex. We are not so honest or so truthful in personal dealings as we were once proud to be.*

There had been ample evidence of impropriety over the past few years. One had been uncomfortably close to the Rector when, early in the war, a married farmer, who also served as churchwarden and treasurer of the parish council, fell ill and was compelled to take six month's rest at Knockholt, near Sevenoaks. Instead of passive recuperation he was found to be regularly commuting into London in order to conduct an affair, for which he was later divorced. Parish council minutes record first his 'unavoidable absence' and, later on, his discreet replacement.

Handled with less discretion was the sensational divorce case which made the society papers in 1943. The Honourable Peter Montefiore Samuel had married in 1939 Miss Deirdre du Barry, the daughter of a Canadian businessman. Her family seemed to change their names whenever it suited – she was originally Vera du Laney, or sometimes du Lavey, and her father Thomas du Laney often went by the name of

Thomas Kent. In any case, while living at Tiffenden Manor, and despite the provision of a handsome £250 income per year, Mrs Samuel committed adultery with a serviceman who by 1943 had been killed on active service. Her husband, himself in service, was granted a divorce – and in stark contrast to his spouse's behaviour, was awarded the Military Cross for gallantry in the field and was mentioned in dispatches for his conduct. He became the 4th Viscount Bearsted in 1986.

As to the charge of dishonest and untruthful dealing, there was plenty of that about, but perhaps one High Halden character epitomised it more than most. 57-year-old Tom Batt of Hales Place Cottages was the sort of lovable rogue who would always stand you a pint in the Chequers and for this could always slip out of trouble; a wheeler-dealer who could obtain and sell anything, and neither asked nor invited questions about where it might have come from. He had been at it 'on the side' for years, but in 1943 began to advertise his services, with the result that business took off. Soon he was selling anything from field guns to Singer sewing machines; ladies' bicycles to carpenter's tools. It didn't seem to matter that most had been marked with other people's names.

The kind of scrap that Batt would not have touched was still accumulating on the village dump. A great heap of scrap-iron, tins and bones had lain there for nearly two years, and there was still no sign of it being cleared. When the Ministry of Works announced the long-delayed removal of railings and gates in the parish this spring, many – with justifiable irritation – asked why the dump couldn't be cleared first, before perfectly good iron had to be dismantled? The eventual reply was that the old scrap metal that had been gathered was 'not of sufficient quality for the intended purpose.' This would rumble on and on for the rest of the year, with complaints of revolting smells and rat infestation. Finally, it took a resolution from the doughty ladies of the High Halden WI to make the Ministry sit up and listen. They were strongly urged

> ... *to speed up the removal of waste from dumps in the villages, as they were harbouring vast quantities of rats, which were a serious menace to food supply and to the health of the community. Moving the resolution, the High Halden delegate said that it was a question which interested everyone in the villages. They had been urged to save tins and bones, but they were simply lying about in untidy, unhealthy dumps, which were a nuisance. 'We want them removed. Do the Government want the things or don't they?' she asked amid applause.*

Within a few months all the local village dumps had been cleared and closed for good, with Lady Geddes asking for volunteers to make up local collections instead.

In the spring, certain local landowners were quietly approached by government officials, and told that they would be required to allow a pipeline to be laid along a small corridor of their land. This work was important for the war effort, they were told, and it would be best not to ask questions, or mention the fact to anyone else. The disruption would not last long, the ground surface would be made good, and they would be fully compensated for any crops lost in the laying of the pipe. Though some were less happy about it than others, every landowner demurred – they had no alternative.

This was no ordinary pipeline. It was part of the most ambitious engineering project yet known, perceived to be vital in winning the war – and High Halden played a small but crucial part. PLUTO – later given the backronyms 'Pipeline Under The Ocean' or 'Pipeline Underwater Transportation of Oil' – was the ingenious means of suppling the Allied invasion forces with vital fuel for their eventual advance through Europe. The project in fact consisted of two pipelines: BAMBI was to run from Shanklin on the Isle of Wight to Normandy, and would be laid across the bed of the Channel as soon as Allied forces had established a beachhead and made it safe to do so. DUMBO would run from Dungeness to Pas-de-Calais, and would come later, once the invaders had pressed north. To reach Dungeness though, trenches needed to be dug and DUMBO run from the refinery at Walton-on-Thames. On its way to the coast, a small stretch of it ran through High Halden.

The work of digging and laying the pipe from Walton-on-Thames to Dungeness – a distance of 72 miles – took six weeks in the summer of 1943. The line bisected a small part of the south-western corner of High Halden parish as it passed out of, and then back into, Tenterden borough. It entered the parish just east of St Michaels village, between Little Harbourne and Pope House Farms. Crossing the Ashford Road at the point where Hallmark Farm is today, it thus crossed the parish boundary and back into Tenterden.

By April construction work had also finished on the airfield but there was little prospect of it being used for the invasion of Europe in the near future. Instead, and to the disappointment of many children, the site was put 'on standby' and the land was temporarily released back to the farmers for grazing. RAF High Halden was to stand idle, in terms of combat operations, for the next six months.

The presence of an air force in High Halden that spring would have brought comfort to many. On Wednesday 24th March, Ashford had suffered a terrible blow which some in High Halden witnessed at a distance. At 10.03am around fifteen Focke-Wulf 190 fighter-bombers approached the town from the south-east, aiming primarily for the vital railway works. Here they dropped several bombs and then went on an indiscriminate rampage, bombing and machine-gunning the town centre and residential streets. Fifty-one people were killed and a further 154 wounded – 76 of whom seriously.

In terms of civilian deaths, it was the worst toll of any single raid on a Kent town during the war, and was part of the new Luftwaffe tactic of 'tip and run' that had also seen the southern part of Tenterden machine-gunned in December 1942. High Halden had received occasional stray rounds from dogfights, but nothing of this nature – yet. Larger towns were still the key targets, and plans were drawn up to evacuate Ashford to outlying villages if the raids continued. 200 townspeople –rising to 250 later in the year – were scheduled to be billeted in High Halden, with a reception point to be set up on the village green. But while the skies above Ashford saw plenty more activity, a raid of this severity never occurred again, and the plan was not put into action.

It made the necessity of a nurse in High Halden seem all the more important, and in July a fundraising drive was launched to raise £500 to provide a car for the service. The Girl Guides contributed nearly a quarter of the target. But Tenterden's Horticultural Society really took up the mantle of this worthy cause, and organised a whist drive, a bazaar and rummage sale, and a huge fete at Hales Place which included a dog show, produce competition, fancy dress parade and the exhibition of some of Tenterden's oldest and rarest relics: a copy of William Caxton's 1482 *Polychronicon*, various council documents from the Middle Ages, and the 16th century parish registers from St Mildred's church.

The following month, in far-off Thailand, 26-year-old **Gunner James ('Jim') Ebenezer Robert Wright** was ailing in a Japanese prisoner-of-war camp. His unit, the 85th Anti-Tank Regiment, was racked with tropical diseases and he finally succumbed to his illness on Saturday 7th August. His widowed mother Mary, living at 'Pantiles' on the Woodchurch Road, was not notified of his death until hostilities in Europe had ended nearly two years later.

The evening of Wednesday 15th September saw the return of enemy activity to a wide area of the Weald with Tenterden at its epicentre. A later investigation identified and plotted the courses of two enemy aircraft that night: one bombed Rolvenden Layne and Benenden; the other Smarden and Pluckley. But it seems the investigators either plotted one incompletely, or that there was at least one other aircraft in the vicinity, as further bombs fell between the two known bomber paths, west of Tenterden, and around the Biddenden-High Halden border.

At around 10pm a cluster of incendiary bombs fell at Stede Quarter, just inside Biddenden parish. An oat stack and some small outbuildings, were set on fire, but the local military soon arrived to extinguish them. One soldier burned his hand in the effort – and is thus recorded as the only casualty of the incident. These fires were witnessed in the early hours by a couple cycling back to High Halden from Tenterden, who years later placed the location as Durrants Green – but this incident at Stede Quarter is the only one to fit the circumstances they describe. Another container of 27 unignited incendiaries landed in a field north of The Grove, just behind what is now the Millfield estate, and was discovered at noon the following day.

Ten minutes after the firebombs had lit up the sky, at 10.10pm, a huge 1,000-kg bomb fell at Thurston Farm – what is now Marlands Farm, just inside the High Halden boundary. The massive explosion blew a crater 65 feet wide – had it fallen one mile to the south-east, in the village centre, the consequences would have been dreadful. As it was, it hit open ground, and the only material damage caused was to a farm cottage, which sustained a cracked chimney.

Mystery surrounds why the area was targeted. Bombs fell around Wittersham Road station, which was not a location of significance, and investigators drew a similar blank at Pluckley and Smarden. There was almost a full moon that night and visibility was good. The only reasonable explanation was that a few careless lights were showing somewhere in the neighbourhood.

A consequence of the Beveridge Report was that, throughout 1943, a sharper lens was turned on the issue of social deprivation. School attendance cases continued to be heard, with the same names cropping up each time, and it was seen that there was a strong correlation between a low living standard and a low rate of school attendance. One such case in High Halden that came to court in October was that of, in the words of the press, a 'mother's shocking neglect' of her six children:

> *The NSPCC inspector called on July 5th and found the house in a terrible condition. The children's bedding was filthy, the food in a horrible condition and furniture supplied by the NSPCC seemed to have disappeared. Defendant occupied a four-roomed bungalow. Five children slept in one room.*
>
> *After the headmistress of High Halden had visited the bungalow, the NSPCC [again] supplied furniture... On October 1st... Dr Tomlinson inspected and his report stated the conditions were appalling and two of the children had rickets. Of four chairs supplied by the society, one had been burnt and the others thrown into a pond.*

It seemed that the mother frequented pubs, leaving her eldest children in charge of the younger ones, and thus preventing them from attending school.

But it was recognised that schools might also have a part to play in alleviating the problem. Thanks to the privations of war, a generation of children were in danger of growing up malnourished. It therefore became the duty of a school's Local Education Authority to provide free school milk and lunches for every pupil. The milk arrived first, in characteristic bottles – holding one-third of a pint – that would become familiar to every British schoolchild over the next thirty years. In winter the crate would be placed on top of the small classroom's stove to defrost, with the result that the milk turned sickly and warm – putting many children off school milk for life.

In time a purpose-built kitchen would be built for each school, but in the interim schools were instructed to make their own lunchtime arrangements. The only realistic option in High Halden was to use the Memorial Hall, which had a small canteen with a coal-fired stove suitable for the purpose. This would take longer to set in motion, but the new arrangement was announced to begin at the start of 1944.

In the late summer came the news that RAF High Halden would be put back into operation – but not with British airmen. It was instead given over to the United States Ninth Air Force as an intended base for squadrons of Thunderbolt fighter-bombers. These heavily-loaded aircraft required more specific facilities than the RAF had envisaged when first building the airfield – most crucially, the main runway was too short, and would need to be extended. Therefore from November onwards USAAF engineers and workmen set up camp in a field adjacent to Harris Wood in Middle Quarter, in order to make the necessary improvements.

The presence of Americans in High Halden was momentous, and much valuable testimony comes from Gwendoline (Gwen) Turner, then a 14-year-old pupil of the Ashford Commercial School living at Sunningdale, Middle Quarter – a couple of hundred yards from the USAAF camp – whose reminiscences were recorded by BBC Radio Kent in the 1990s. She and her mother had a tempered reaction to the new arrivals, resenting the disruption and noise to the neighbourhood, and the fact that security in the area was tightened, with the sentry posts of military policemen set up at every nearby road junction. One – at the three-went-way between Little Acorn Farm and Summerleaze Cottage – was particularly problematic, being manned by an over-amorous pest who confirmed an unfortunate stereotype of American servicemen. One time Gwen was cycling past, carrying a can of milk from nearby Shawlands Farm:

> *I absolutely dreaded going by whenever he was on duty… he would come marching out across the road… He succeeded in throwing me off rather badly once, and I had got the milk in the can: spilt nearly all of it. So I thought, 'Right, he's asked for it… he might as well have the rest of this can.' It did resist his activities a little bit after that, as far as I was concerned. But… there was a 15-year-old girl just up the road… she lived nearer to the aerodrome, and she didn't mind at all.*

After another incident, in which Gwen fended off his attentions by hitting him with her gas-mask, her younger brother Stanley began to accompany her. Despite this, the younger children 'were thrilled to bits' with the new arrivals, scrounging sweets and attending film-shows at the camp, which the soldiers advertised with posters stuck to the telegraph poles. As Gwen acknowledged:

> *... one advantage of living in the middle of that camp was their generosity. They sympathized because my father was away; they were away from their folk, and so if they could give us anything, they did... We had dried peaches galore, powdered milk, and powdered egg – which wasn't very nice... but you would eat it if you was hungry.*

In return, Mrs Turner sent her old newspapers up to the camp for the servicemen to read, and offered to write to their wives back home in the States. Several airmen were also invited to the family home for meals, although some of their habits weren't appreciated:

> *They chewed chewing-gum the whole time. You never saw an American with his eyes open and he wasn't chewing. My mother hated it; so did I, because of course they used to stick it under the legs of the tables and the chairs. She told them off for having it, 'You can get rid of that,' and then they'd hide it up somewhere, thinking they were going to help themselves to it later*

> *on… They'd stick it underneath the table, even lift up*
> *[the tablecloth] and stick it on the inner hem, anywhere*
> *they could think of.*

This November the Americans introduced the Turner family to Thanksgiving, of which they'd had no notion before. They also saw black soldiers for the first time, though were less than impressed with the way they were made to do jobs their white colleagues didn't want to do. In a few months time, on particularly hot days, they would be seen driving the fuel tankers around the lanes:

> *It got very hot driving those oil tankers… my brother*
> *saw one way up a lane one day, and he was sunbathing,*
> *laying on top of this hot tanker, sun belting down on*
> *him! My brother just couldn't get over that. I felt they*
> *were really unkind to them, but thank goodness over the*
> *years it's all changed, hasn't it?*

Back in November 1943, warmth was very much on the mind of Rev. Champion, whose church was pitifully heated by oil stoves that contributed, he felt sure, to the falling-off of numbers attending Sunday worship. It added up to a rather chilly and uncomfortable welcome for the Archbishop of Canterbury when he arrived to conduct a Confirmation service, which was the final straw. A quote of £355 for a new heating system was obtained, plus the cost of building a boilerhouse on the north-east side of the church, and as ever the church finances alone would not meet it. Charitable giving was everywhere yet becoming stretched ever more thinly this winter: £33 7s 5d for Poppy Day; £4 15s for the Red Cross through a WI toy sale; £4 3s 9d for the Women's Land Army Benevolent Fund.

One whose activities were less than charitable was local spiv Tom Batt, whose dealings caught up with him on Saturday 20th November when the police raided his home and found several lots of stolen goods. The first was a shotgun belonging to Challock Home Guard, taken from a shed three weeks previously. Next was a magneto, missing from a tractor at Sevington, and a selection of tools stolen from a store at Willesborough in February. Further investigation found that he had recently sold three bicycles to a gentleman in Battersea – all of which had been unlawfully liberated from their owners. Batt was charged with receiving stolen goods and tried at Ashford on Thursday 9th December. He managed to wriggle out of the first charge – the Challock shotgun had been given to him by a known drunkard, and Batt did not know it was stolen – but pleaded guilty to the rest and asked that several other offences be taken into consideration:

> *Receiving a magneto, valued £11 13s, the property of Kent War Agricultural Committee; a magneto, valued £14 4s, the property of Alec Hickman; another magneto, valued £5, the property of the War Agricultural Committee; a gent's cycle, valued £6, the property of A.W. Lake; and another cycle, valued £8.*

Being in unlawful possession of Army stores, blankets, telescope, volt meter, brushes, jersey, vests, pants, treacle, jam, 5,000 round .22 ammunition, total value, 50 g[ui]n[ea]s.

Unlawfully possessing 5,000 rounds ammunition, not being the holder of a firearms certificate.

Batt was sentenced to a year's imprisonment and a fine of £100 plus costs. Several of his associates, convicted of ancillary offences, were fined or given shorter terms of imprisonment. The chairman of the Bench remarked that such offences were 'of a serious nature and of a character likely to impede the war effort.' With Tom Batt now out of the picture for a while, High Halden was to be just a little less lawless.

1944

TOWARDS THE END of 1943, the Youth Hostelling Association purchased Turks Head Farm, on the border with Biddenden, in order to convert the farmhouse into a youth hostel. This was done in fairly short order and it opened in the second week of January 1944, with couple Will and Joan Rutter acting as Wardens. Over the next few months they welcomed hundreds of young backpackers who were given accommodation in return for labour on the hundred acres of land, and the contribution of 2/6d each towards an evening meal. Rev. Champion was full of praise:

> *Dozens of jobs are done by these young people: planting, hoeing, harvesting, haymaking, hedging, ditching, threshing and so on. Work for all; but also rambles and cycle rides are arranged, as well as visits to other farms and farming demonstrations. It is difficult to exaggerate the possibilities of good arising from this introduction of town-dwellers to the actual experience of rural life...*

Another innovation early this year was the long-awaited opening of the school canteen in the Memorial Hall. At noon each day, a long crocodile of pupils would leave the school and walk up Church Hill, where the smell of freshly-baked bread from Ledger's shop would strengthen the appetite. The tables at the hall were set out by one or two older children, who had left a few minutes earlier. Somehow, despite shortages, the cooked meals were generous, plentiful and nutritious, and there is little doubt that for some village children it provided their only chance to have a decent meal.

The American engineers finished their work on the air base in early April – the most significant change being the extension of the main runway's southern end by another thousand feet, bringing it over Pot Kiln Lane and into fields to the south. Then in the afternoon of Thursday 13th April, the 358th USAAF Fighter Group – made of the 365th, 366th and 367th Squadrons – arrived. High Halden was designated as Station AAF-411 (code HH).

The P-47 Thunderbolt was a versatile fighter-bomber which was powerful and remained flyable even after sustaining heavy damage. It functioned both as an escort fighter for heavier bombers, and as a ground-attack bomber in its own right. As such it was widely used in the Allied campaign and would come to play a vital role in the liberation of Europe. However it was one of the heaviest fighters of its time, with a particularly wide fuselage, and could neither climb fast nor turn tightly. Once mastered, with a pilot who thought tactically, it performed well – but to less experienced airmen it took time to get to grips with.

Consequently, for the next few weeks USAAF High Halden was a dangerous place to be. During the first ten days of air operations – from Thursday 20th April onwards – there were seven recorded accidents, either during take-off, landing, or taxiing. Then on Friday 19th May a Thunderbolt, piloted by Lieutenant Ed Maclean of the 377th Squadron based at Headcorn, suffered an engine failure and made a forced landing half a mile north of the High Halden airfield which caused the plane to be written off. Over the next seven weeks there would be five further take-off accidents, three landing accidents and one taxiing accident.

When they weren't causing damage to their own aircraft or airfield, the American vehicles churned up the roads and verges all over the parish, leading Tenterden Rural District Council to seek a grant for their repair from the Ministry of War Transport. Also disruptive was the fact that Pot Kiln Lane was closed to all traffic while operations were underway, necessitating a diversion via Harris Lane and Middle Quarter instead.

Since the previous July, when they invaded Sicily, and then the mainland in September, Allied forces had been advancing northwards through Italy. By early 1944 they had reached the Gustav line, a defensive fallback running southwest-northeast through the mountainous terrain of central Italy, between Rome and Naples. Over five months the Allies attempted four assaults on the monastery at the summit of Monte Cassino, being used as a fortified German observation post to direct fire on to the Allies in the lowlands below. It was on the last of these assaults, on Monday 15th May, that **Colour Serjeant Peter Colohan Ettridge**, a career soldier of the Queen's Own Royal West Kent Regiment, died aged 27. His wife Phyllis, whom he had married in 1939, was a local girl from the Burden family, born in Bethersden and living in High Halden with a three-year-old daughter at the time of her husband's death. Monte Cassino was captured and the Gustav Line broken, opening the road to Rome; but it was a truly Pyrrhic victory, with 55,000 Allied casualties. Three weeks later, on Tuesday 6th June, D-Day heralded the invasion of Europe and the start of the long and desperate battle of attrition through Normandy and the road to Paris and from thence, eventually, to Berlin.

Back home, there was a push of a different kind and, arguably, this battle would be harder-won. A few weeks earlier High Halden's WI had discussed with indignation the fact that not one woman served on the parish council, which had not sat since 1940. With the resumption of meetings one of the Misses Richford of Orchard House was delegated to write a letter to the council drawing their attention to this matter: she made the observation that during wartime, in line with the prevailing attitude, there should be more opportunities for women to serve, not fewer. The letter was discussed in the May meeting and Miss Richford was advised that a candidate – whatever their sex – may put themselves forward to be co-opted on to the council at the next meeting, where there were three vacancies available.

Sensing a victory for their cause, on Wednesday 7th June three ladies nominated by the WI – Mrs Fowler, Mrs Rofe and Miss Morris – duly put their names forward in the expectation that at least one of them would be elected. They were to be sadly disappointed and their organisation outraged when all three seats were filled by men. It was a result that left many embittered towards the parish council, which after four years in abeyance was seen by some to have become an irrelevance.

The council had problems of its own, however. Their only rental property, on Poorsfield, had been damaged by nearby bombs and was now being shaken to pieces by troop movements and aircraft in the neighbourhood. Additionally – or perhaps because of it – Young Sam Adams had not paid any rent since September 1942. It had not been pursued since then, and so he had not bothered, building up a debt he found unable to meet. When in June 1944 the council finally called it in, his cheque bounced twice and solicitors' letters were written – but Adams dodged them all by dying suddenly of meningitis, aged 38, leaving his sister Maggie to take over the property and clear the debt.

Rumours of 'Hitler's Secret Weapon' had spread for some time, and in the early hours of 13th June, it was unleashed against Britain. It was first seen by observers on top of a

Martello tower at Dymchurch: expelling a long plume of angry orange flame, and making a characteristic droning noise. This was the *Vergeltungswaffe Eins* – Revenge Weapon One, or V-1 – with which Hitler would make a last-ditch attempt to batter London into submission. These weapons, originally termed 'pilotless aircraft' and then 'flying bombs' became known as the 'doodlebug' (to the British public) or 'buzz bomb' (to the American soldiers).

It was a fiendish and fearsome weapon. Launched from sites in northern France, the V-1 was aimed directly at the centre of London at 400 miles per hour, carrying 850kg of high explosive and just enough fuel to meet its target. Onlookers listened for its drone and prayed for it to pass overhead, as once the fuel ran out it would dip forwards, dragged down by its weighted nose, and plummet to earth. One of three fuses could set it off: an electrical one as soon as it impacted the ground; a slightly delayed one to allow the nose to penetrate further into the ground; or if these failed, a timer fuse that would ignite two hours after launch.

Many were shot down into the Channel by the anti-aircraft guns along the coast. But many more got through to be met by fighter pilots with instructions to bring them down before their reached the capital. In practice, this meant into (relatively) sparsely-populated Kent. And it so happened that, taking into account the point at which a V-1 was sighted approaching the coast from the south-east, and the time it took a patrolling aircraft to catch up with it, the two tended to meet over the Tenterden area. A post-war reckoning showed that the Tenterden district received more V-1 hits (238) than any other, with Ashford a distant second (184).

They were not particularly difficult to shoot down: as long as it was already patrolling the air, a Spitfire or Hurricane could match the speed of a V-1, and its constant course without deviation made it easy prey. Sometimes all it took was a gentle tap on the wing, and its own propulsion sent it hurtling to the ground. Locals soon learned to fear the doodlebug. On Saturday 17th June, one crashed near the sanatorium at Benenden (now Benenden Hospital), causing widespread damage, demolishing a farmhouse, and killing three members of the same family.

Although its people did not realise it for some time, High Halden suffered its first losses in this new wave of terror the following day, in the most serious V-1 attack of the war. On Sunday 18th June, at 11.20am, a flying bomb scored a direct hit on the Guards' Chapel at Wellington Barracks, off Birdcage Walk in Westminster. The concrete roof caved in and walls collapsed on the congregation attending the morning service inside. 121 people, a mix of servicemen and civilians, were killed, with a further 141 severely injured. It took days to retrieve all the bodies, and longer still to identify them, but in due course it was confirmed that among the dead were 53-year-old **Violet Maud ('Diana') Wall** and her husband 43-year-old **Captain Leslie Edwin**

Gordon Wall – the daughter and son-in-law of Susan Jackson of Haffenden.

Later that day, at 4.50pm, and with the village still unaware of events in London, the first V-1 to crash in the parish came down on the USAAF airfield. Howard Millen, then 15 years old and living at Wagstaff Farm, witnessed the diving doodlebug on a collision course with a pile of stacked-up bombs:

> *It was heading straight for them, when it hit a great big oak, which was blown to smithereens. It was a near miss, and dust from the blast covered everything. All the guns on the airfield were firing and the horses bolted halfway to Headcorn. There has never been a firework display like it.*

Much to the ARP unit's frustration, no further information could be gained from the American authorities as to the incident; and it was the same story five days later, at 9.05pm on Thursday 23rd June, when a second V-1 also came down on the base. No-one is believed to have been killed in either incident. But the Americans were certainly wary of the new threat, and as Howard Millen relates, they did not hesitate to use all the ground firepower they could muster at the airfield when they saw the infernal machines approaching. An American colonel, Thomas Glass, later recalled making an inspection of the High Halden operation:

> *On the way there, I observed the large number of barrage balloons along the V-1 buzz bomb route to London. At High Halden, I observed how methodical the Germans were: at 25 minutes and again at 55 minutes after the hour, a buzz bomb would come over. You could have set your watch by them!*

It added up to an already-dangerous situation for the men of the USAAF, as their air operations in France were ramping up. On Thursday 22nd June Lieutenant Bob Kelso of 379th Squadron (at High Halden) crash-landed his Thunderbolt in an orchard two miles north of the High Halden airfield – while the official log gives engine failure as the cause, anecdotal evidence tells that his aircraft was also badly shot up with enemy flak across the water. Still the advance through Normandy was steadily inching its way forward, and very shortly the operations at USAAF High Halden would be moved over to France itself.

During the last week of June three anti-aircraft gun units were established in High Halden parish to help deal with the V-1 menace. The first, on Saturday 24th, was in the corner of a field opposite Brick House Farm; the second, the following day, was north of Brickyard Farm, behind the junction of the Ashford Road and Cripple Hill. Lastly, on Wednesday 28th June, one was set up in a field at America Farm – now known as Sportsman Farm.

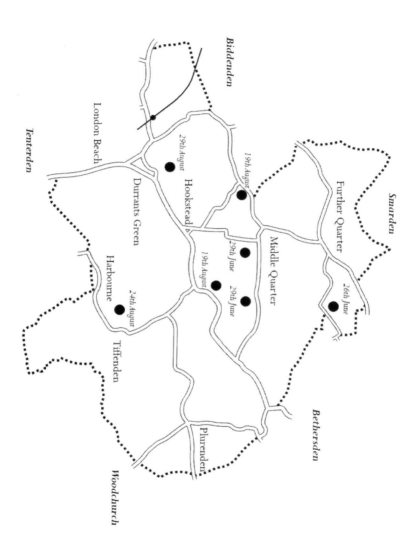

Confirmed V-1 flying bomb strikes, 1944.

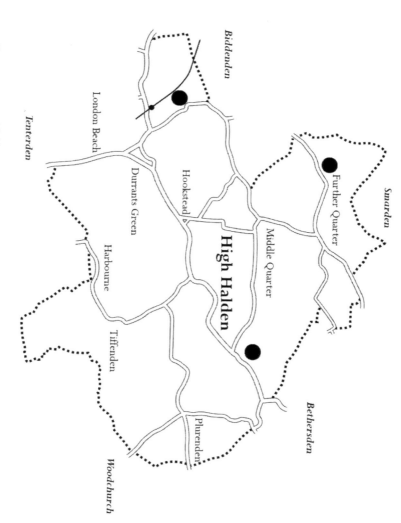

Anti-aircraft gun positions, 1944.

Little surprise, then, that anti-aircraft fire brought down High Halden's first V-1 on civilian soil, at 4am on Monday 26th June, which crashed south-east of Potkiln Farm, just north of Green Lane. It was later this day that Rev. Champion referred to the flying bomb threat as a 'destructive and pernicious nuisance while it lasts.' Three days later, on Thursday 29th, Middle Quarter suffered two hits very close to each other along the line of Cripple Hill, both brought down by British fighter planes: the first, at 4.40pm, fell just east of Ramstile Farm, breaking windows and blowing a crater 30 feet wide; the second, at 10.20pm, only 750 yards west of the first, making a similar crater south of where Greenacres Farm is today.

Just up the road, on that very same day the Americans began to leave their High Halden base, taking their Thunderbolts over to a new forward posting at Cretteville, on the Cherbourg peninsula in Normandy. It was a gradual process and operations would still be flown from the site for another few weeks, but Gwen Turner's younger siblings were disappointed as their sweets and film shows came to an end. There was some solace, however, in the discovery of a large stash of tinned food in Harris Wood which the 'very wasteful' Americans had buried before they left.

The Turner family still had the particular worry of V-1s:

> *The doodlebugs frightened the life out of us. One half-*
> *term, when I came cycling home, this thing went over*

*and little did I know, it killed the first lady and her
fourteen-year-old daughter that my mum ever knew
when she came to Kent. Only enough between the two
of them to put in one coffin.*

In a reversal of 1939, a scheme for evacuating the children
of the district was hastily drawn up, with Tenterden
redesignated from a reception to an evacuation area. It was
arranged for children of school age whose parents wished
them to leave to go to billets in Dulverton in Somerset, a
market town on Exmoor, and others to Monmouth just over
the Welsh border, and this operation began on Tuesday 18th
July. It is unclear precisely how many children left from
High Halden, and estimates range from ten to twenty.

At virtually the same moment as the first exhausted refugees
were being shown to their billets in the Westcountry,
11.02pm, a Lancaster bomber from 460 Squadron of the
Royal Australian Air Force took off from RAF Binbrook in
Lincolnshire. Its mission, along with 170 other bombers,
was to attack an oil plant in Gelsenkirchen in western
Germany, an objective successfully accomplished. On the
return journey, at 1.45am on Wednesday 19th July, the
plane crashed at Roggel in the Netherlands with the loss of
all crew. On board as Flight Engineer was 30-year-old
Sergeant William James Cecil Cambridge, the son of
Diana Wall who had died at Wellington Barracks one month
previously. In the space of four weeks in this terrible

summer, Susan Jackson of Haffenden had lost her daughter, son-in-law and grandson.

The following four weeks, though, saw relative calm in High Halden as it managed to evade the flying bomb menace. Nonetheless there was constant news of incidents within neighbouring parishes in all directions. A mother and her teenage daughter died at Rolvenden; their house obliterated – though her recollection is doubtful, this was most likely the incident to which Gwen Turner refers, above. A woman at Appledore and a teenage boy at Biddenden were both shot to death in the machine-gun fire of British fighters. Woodchurch village centre was hit, rendering many houses unsafe for habitation, though mercifully nobody was killed or seriously injured. In two of the worst incidents of the period, two houses in Smarden suffered direct hits, killing five members of one family and four of another, including several children. Benenden also suffered terribly with nine deaths: as well as the early incident near the Sanatorium, six others died in further attacks, including a teenage boy, two soldiers, and two itinerant agricultural workers. The fact that High Halden was spared any casualties at home during this period was purely a matter of good fortune.

Especially so, given that in its early stages hundreds of heavily-armed Americans and then anti-aircraft units were actively trying to bring the bombs down – and then, for a short while in August the airfield (now RAF High Halden again) hosted Meteor jet fighters of 616 Squadron as part of

Operation Diver, the British countermeasures against the V-1 menace. Though based at Manston, the aircraft of 616 Squadron frequently landed at High Halden to refuel, and from Monday 14th August they split their base between the two stations. The following evening, **Flight Sergeant Donald Arthur Gregg** flew to High Halden to take up his duties but, unable to find the airfield, doubled back and attempted a landing at RAF Ashford, near Great Chart. The engine stalled on approach and he was killed when his Meteor crashed in flames.

This was followed by a further crash at High Halden, two days later, on Thursday 17th August. Pilot Officer Edwin Matthew, of 130 Squadron based at Tangmere, was on patrol against V-1s over High Halden when the crankshaft of his Spitfire broke, causing engine failure. Matthew managed to glide it to a runway of RAF High Halden but overshot the end, coming to rest in a field. The pilot sustained only minor injuries, though his Spitfire was badly damaged. Unbelievably, a similar incident had happened to Matthew in training the previous September, when his Spitfire was forced to belly-land after an engine failure near Waddingham, Lincolnshire.

With so many defenders overheard and on the ground attempting to shoot down the doodlebugs, it was only a matter of time before the village would be thrown back into the war in spectacular fashion. It happened at 2.30pm on Saturday 19th August, when a V-1 crashed and exploded at

Little Robhurst Farm, at a point north of the pond that today lies behind numbers 10 and 12 on the Little Robhurst estate. Back in 1944, this was open grazing land owned by Sydney Read. The blast wave from the explosion killed 16 of his sheep and lambs, and damaged the barns and stables of the farm. 31 buildings in the village centre and out towards Ransley Farm were also affected, with windows shattered and tiles blown off the roofs. In terms of damage, it was High Halden's most destructive incident of the war – yet still, nobody was killed or even injured. A further V-1 crash nine hours later, at 11.30pm, set fire to a cornfield across the road from Thurston Farm (now Marlands Farm), but was quickly extinguished by the fire service.

Woodgate's men were set to work for 'long hours without intermission' to make the damaged houses weatherproof again, and were assisted in their task by Major MacKeleken of the Chequers, who acted as liaison with the military still in the area, and was able to round up further assistance from them. All repairs were temporary 'quick fixes' and would need to be revisited after the war.

So far, all V-1 hits had occurred in the upper part of the parish, north of the A28. The southern part received its only visit at 9.45pm on Thursday 24th August, when a crash just north of Pond Wood damaged around a dozen buildings on the Harbourne Hall and Farm estate. Five days later, on Tuesday 29th August at 12.50pm, came Hitler's last shot at the village when a V-1, brought down by a British fighter, crashed by Trimmer Wood, north of London Beach. The blast wave travelled across the open fields towards Durrants Green and Oak Grove, where four-year-old Pat Moore (Wenbourne) witnessed its effects:

> *My sister and I were in the Morrison shelter in our living room, so we must have heard the bomb coming over. Mother was standing at the front window, looking at the fields over the road. The bomb landed, the blast blew the window in, and the broken glass embedded itself into her arm. Then — I can see it to this day — she slowly lifted her hands up to her head, to check it was still attached to the rest of her.*

Thirteen-year-old Frank Bourne recalled that most of the houses nearby had windows blown in and ceilings brought down. His own mother was standing at the top of their staircase when the explosion blew her right down to the ground floor. It was probably this same blast that caused a weight of plaster to detach from a wall and land on Peter Deacon's grandmother. Apart from the odd bruise neither was hurt, and only the unfortunate Mrs Moore was logged in the ARP record as 'one woman, slightly wounded' — becoming High Halden's only 'home' civilian casualty of the war, and in its very last incident.

This was almost the very last V-1 of the war; the launching sites in northern France began to be overrun by Allied forces on the same day, and the attacks stopped as abruptly as they had started eleven weeks earlier. The threat to High Halden was now over, and the area was barely affected by the impending V-2 rocket menace – the only incident occurred at Benenden the following January, though no-one was hurt.

Just a few miles from these launching sites, in the Pas-de-Calais region of France, were the 11th Hussars of the Royal Armoured Corps, which included 23-year-old **Lieutenant Donald Ashworth Creaton**, the son of a previous vicar of Bethersden. On Sunday 3rd September Lieutenant Creaton was leading a troop through the village of Croisette when he suddenly came across a group of Germans manning an anti-tank gun. According to civilian eyewitnesses, the enemy promptly surrendered while Creaton covered them with his Sten gun. What happened next is uncertain, but when shots rang out, a follow-up troop rounded the corner to see the British soldiers being led off as prisoners of the Germans who had previously surrendered, and Creaton dead on the ground; shot through the head. The war diary records:

> *Lt Creaton had a magnificent record of Troop leading; which had started before the fall of Tunis, carried on all through Italy and since landing in France. He was exceptionally brave and thorough and very accurate in all his reports. His loss was a great blow to all who knew him; he was a first class officer in every respect and most popular. It seems likely that his death was a typical act of German treachery, either it was one of those who had*

surrendered who shot him, or else some unseen enemy on which those who had raised their hands, promptly lowered them and attacked the remainder of the Troop.

Lieutenant Creaton was buried by the road at the point where he fell, and his widowed mother, Marjorie Creaton of Jessamine Cottage, later bought the land to prevent her son's remains being disturbed and moved to a communal cemetery. A monument was erected on the spot which stands to this day. A Military Cross, for which Creaton had been recommended for several actions in August when he saved a soldier from a burning vehicle, knocked out a German 40mm gun and took six prisoners, was posthumously awarded the following March.

Back home, the realisation was sinking in that there would be no further threat to civilians and property, at least around High Halden. In consequence, that autumn's Harvest Festival took on a more heartened tone of thanksgiving than in previous years, to which Rev. Champion alluded when he wrote that 'life in this part of England is returning to a more normal condition than it has known for a long time.' It was therefore all the crueller when Spring Hill, a house almost adjacent to the old mill, accidentally caught fire and burned to the ground on Tuesday 12th September, causing no injuries but the loss of all the possessions of the Stroud family. Master of the house was George Stroud, a Royal Flying Corps hero of the last war, who was teaching in Kenya and had left the house in the care of wife May who had once taught at the village school. She and her children received much sympathy from the village, and being the sister of William Peters Woodgate, the family firm was able to rebuild their property. A further pointer to normality was the decommissioning of RAF High Halden on Friday 15th September, though the land would not be cleared and returned to the farmers until early the following year.

By now it was also deemed safe for the evacuated children to return to the village from the Westcountry, and those who had come to High Halden from the coast to return home as well. Rev. Champion particularly regretted the loss of organist Mr Strong, but hoped that his replacement Mr Hotchkiss would inject some life into the congregation, who persisted in clustering in the back pews of the church and not engaging in the services with sufficient vigour:

> It is amazing how much noise two or three people can make when having a quiet chat; but put the same people in High Halden Church and let them take part in a service in which they are urged to respond — and there is a silence as of the grave!

Another familiar face to return to the village was the incorrigible Tom Batt, after a slightly shortened term of imprisonment. He set up once more at Hales Place Cottages that autumn and within a few weeks was selling an Austin Seven saloon, a Blackstone engine and dynamo, motorised saw bench, an array of guns and a butcher's refrigerator.

One man who would not return was 23-year-old **Captain Peter Leonard Fanning**, the son of Frederick and Patricia Fanning of Crowhurst, by Pope House Farm on the Tenterden road and the nearest home to where Franz Hessel's Messerschmitt had crashed in 1940. Educated at Radley College and The Queen's College, Oxford (during which time he rowed in the 1940 Boat Race which was held unofficially due to war conditions), Peter served with the 5th Battalion of the Coldstream Guards and was in the thick of the Normandy campaign from D-Day onwards, fighting through Bayeux and across northern France. The battalion's war diary gives no specific details as to his death on Saturday 4th November but the objective that day was to advance through woods surrounding the village of Leunen in the Netherlands, which were understood to have been full of elite German parachute divisions. A stray shell is believed to have killed Captain Fanning, who was buried in the nearby cemetery of Venray, the nearest town.

The order for the Home Guard to 'stand down' was given on Saturday 3rd December, and the men were roundly toasted in both the Chequers and the Man of Kent for a 'job well done.' Once their own celebrations were over, they decided to throw a party for the children of the parish, and their very last task of the war – one which none of them had envisaged – was to arrange this for the New Year. More than one old volunteer reckoned that dealing with a hall full of children was a more frightening prospect than anything he may have been called to do over the past four-and-a-half years.

1945

THE THREAT TO the country may have largely lifted, but danger was still present. On Thursday 1st March 49-year-old **Lieutenant-Colonel Clement John Hogbin**, late of the Indian Army in the last war and now the commander of an anti-aircraft battery of the Royal Artillery, was returning from making an inspection outside Hornsea in Yorkshire, where the 145th Heavy Anti-Aircraft Regiment was based. He was accompanied by another officer and two ATS ladies in the army car, which was being driven by one of them, 26-year-old Private Dorothy Smith. On approaching a crossroads near Hornsea Station the car was struck by a lorry, which pushed it twenty yards down the street and into the end of some iron railings which pierced its side, trapping the passengers with severe injuries. Private Smith and 33-year-old Senior Commander Charlotte Clerk-Rattray, a niece of the Duchess of Atholl, died along with Lieutenant-Colonel Hogbin, who before the war had been a well-travelled career soldier, serving in the Far East. But 'home' during the late 1930s and war years was Bridge Farm, High Halden where his wife Elizabeth still managed the poultry farm.

The tracking, hangars, perimeter fences and administration buildings of the airfield had now been removed, but the outline of the runways could still clearly be seen from the air. On Sunday 19th March a B-17 Flying Fortress bomber was badly shot-up over Germany, but managed to make it back to England. It attempted a landing on the runway at High Halden but, with no metal tracking to help support it, the wheels sank into the soft earth and gouged huge channels across several fields. The aircraft remained there for several weeks, until the ground had dried out and hardened, before it could take off again.

April brought the heady anticipation that it would soon be all over, as news came in of the Allied advance towards Berlin. Rev. Champion and the parochial church council set to work, formulating their plans for the announcement of Victory in Europe. Every available ringer was instructed to stand ready to come and ring the church bells 'at a moment's notice' – if necessary they would be collected by car by the rector or his verger Robert Coultham. If the announcement was in the morning, the bells would ring at noon, with a short thanksgiving service at 12.30pm. If the news arrived in the afternoon, it would be six o'clock for 6.30pm.

The announcement was made late on Monday 7th May, but somewhere along the line the plans changed, and the bells rang out at 6pm the following day for a service that evening. Rev. Champion later reflected:

> *A large number of you came to give thanks to God on*
> *VE-Day and the following Sunday. It was indeed a*
> *happy climax to the long-drawn-out waiting and*
> *working of Wardens, Special Constables, Fire-guards,*
> *Home Guard, Red Cross and Ambulance units and so*
> *on, that all should meet together in a fellowship of*
> *thankful acknowledgement to Almighty God that we*
> *owe to Him our deliverance and our victory.*

This was, however, the only official celebration to be found in High Halden on VE-Day; the councils preferring to wait until hostilities had ended in the Far East before committing to an official event. However, the two pubs were filled, and others made the journey either to Tenterden or Ashford, where impromptu rejoicing broke out in the streets. There were plenty of wobbly bicycle journeys back from either town in the early hours of the morning.

Barely a week had passed when the council announced plans for the returning servicemen, and their fulfilment of the promise of 'homes fit for heroes.' Eleven prefabricated houses were to be built at Hookstead, on land purchased for £250 from the current occupier Rev. Morrice Lionel Man – a former vicar of Tenterden. These 'prefabs' were envisaged to last ten years; the ones at Hookstead saw nearly 30 years' use, being demolished in the mid-1970s.

The men of the armed forces began to return home; the time determined by their whereabouts and length of service. Each time an arrival was expected the flags would come out again, this time focused around the home of his wife or mother, with neighbours clapping and cheering. There was no such relief for Mrs Wright of Pantiles, who learned in June of the death of her son Jim two years previously (see p.115). As the veterans returned they brought back diseases from their travels, and in the summer a wave of dysentery broke over the area, particularly affecting infants and the elderly. Shortly afterwards a throat ailment took hold, which was so severe that it posed a threat to life. Inevitably, through her constant contact with children, the village headmistress Miss Rossiter was badly affected – she managed to recover but her constitution was badly weakened.

With the atomic bombing of Hiroshima and Nagasaki that brought about the surrender of Japan, VJ-Day was declared on 15th August. This was also the day chosen for Rev. Champion to call an emergency meeting of the parochial church council, at which he announced his resignation, to take up a post in Sri Lanka.

> It seems to me very fitting that, after all the chances and changes of the years through which we have passed together in this village, the closing note of my ministry should be one of thanksgiving... not only for the great deliverance which we share with our fellow-countrymen, but also for special blessings, both material and spiritual – having been spared casualties and grievous damage, being allowed to carry on our

avocations in quietness and hoping (alas with some few exceptions) to receive our loved ones home safe and sound, living on the whole a harmonious and unquarrelsome life with many instances of brotherly kindness and mutual helpfulness...

While this sombre meeting was taking place in the schoolroom, the local pubs were once again filled with revellers. But there was still no official celebration, as everyone had taken by surprise at the suddenness of the Japanese surrender. Tenterden Rural District Council hurriedly sent a letter to each parish council suggesting a 'public tea for the children and their mothers and old people' to be held in each village, of which 'all reasonable expenditure' would be met. An emergency parish council meeting held two days after VJ-Day appointed Ledger's to undertake the catering for 250 people, asked the WI and Mothers' Union to provide helpers, and fixed the date of the party as Saturday 1st September at 4pm. A week beforehand, more details were fixed, with Mr C.S. Banks confirmed to put on a film show (for £1, the cost of hiring the films) and 'Devla' the magician booked to perform a 20-minute show at £2 12s 6d. Ledger's Stores had also taken delivery of the much-valued extra food coupons, specially produced for the occasion.

On the appointed day High Halden's Memorial Hall hosted a party it had not seen for years. The caterers surpassed themselves with an unforgettable tea full of sweet treats.

The children toasted the peace with bottles of milk donated by various farms. Sports were held on Hookstead Green with running races up and down the roads. Finally, as darkness fell a mass of fireworks lit up the sky – a spectacular rejoinder from those who, for the past six years, had only looked upwards with fear.

Woodgate's were kept busy in High Halden for several years, removing their temporary repairs to bomb-damaged properties – such as Ransley Cottages and Church Farm – and making them permanent. They were also called upon to refurbish Hathewolden Grange after its rather heavy-handed occupation by the military. One property they were not called to work upon was Poorsfield, the repairs to which would have been too extensive for the council to fund. Instead it was agreed to sell off the house and land – the last remaining charitable property in the hands of the parish council – and this was done in April 1947. The building was demolished soon afterwards and a new property stands on the site.

By then the parish council had experienced a substantial and heartening change. From the humiliation of 1944, when no female candidates were elected, within two short years they formed the majority of councillors – five women to three men. It has been said that the end of the war marked the start of the emancipation of women, and here we see it reflected at parish level: the old guard had been almost entirely swept away, either by death, resignation or defeat at the polls.

One such loss was Charles Brown of Hales Place, who had died in December 1944. After the departure of the heavy army vehicles six months earlier, leaving it in an undesirable state, he had bought Hookstead Green and donated it to Tenterden Rural District Council to be used in perpetuity as a children's playground. The Council initially showed gratitude, then apathy by letting the land sit idle for five years, then meanness by telling the parish council they should bear the cost for putting it in order, and finally greed by attempting to build two cottages on the site – only averted by an intervention from solicitors instructed by Mr Brown's widow. By 1949 the land had been put right and playground equipment installed, with the facility in place and much enjoyed to this day.

By this time the Rural District Council that held sway over so many lives had moved from Tenterden and taken up new headquarters at Halden House, where it would remain until the council was subsumed into that of Ashford Borough Council in 1974. It is they who took on responsibility for High Halden's council housing, both in the pre-war Hookstead development and the subsequent 36 homes at the Chennells in 1947 and a further 38 at Greenside in 1954. In the immediate post-war years many improvements were made to substandard housing – including the demolition of some – and water and electricity services were extended to the whole parish.

Rev. Arthur Champion left for Sri Lanka in January 1946, and spend several years in ministry there before returning home for retirement in Surrey. He died in 1964, and is buried in the family plot in Suffolk. His dedicated churchwarden and the bastion of civil defence during the war years, William Woodgate, died in 1952. His employers at Woodgate's constructed the lych-gate, forming the main entrance to the churchyard, in his memory.

Just to the rear of the lych-gate is the war memorial, to which a base plaque commemorating the fallen from the Second World War was added a few years after its ending. The last name is of 29-year-old **Fusilier Leslie Wilfred Carpenter** of the 8th Battalion of the Royal Fusiliers (City of London Regiment. The unit's war diary records their presence in Kavouri, on the western coast of Greece, but gives no details as to this soldier's death. The battalion had just returned from a tour of the Middle East, including peacekeeping duties in Palestine. Carpenter's widow Elsie lived in Tenterden during the war, but had moved to High Halden by the time of her husband's death.

Barring the occasional scraps of nondescript old metal, there is no longer any outward sign of the airfield used by the RAF and USAAF in the latter stages of the war. But a closer look at this peaceful, pastoral landscape reveals that for long stretches the field boundaries are not marked by established hedgerows but newer post and spile fences, and in the hot, dry conditions of high summer the scars of the old runway can still be traced from the air. Finds are usually turned up by metal detectorists: in 2018 the identification tag of a US airman was recovered, and returned to its then-95-year-old owner in the States.

Snippets and half-stories, sometimes much-distorted over the years, suggest events that were never entered into the official record. Such as the suggestion that a spy was found signalling to enemy bombers to target Harbourne Hall – or the proposal that the reason a house's roof-timbers were newer at one end was that they had been repaired after an undocumented V-1 had exploded nearby. It is unfair and indeed impossible to say there is no truth in these; simply that they cannot be verified by contemporaneous documentary proof which, for the historian, must take precedence over hearsay. Nonetheless, they all add up to the picture of life in these unique, fraught and sometimes desperate times. These stories never die: they also reflect how much those six years of war, of now nearly eighty years ago, have influenced and continue to influence our lives and collective consciousness as a nation today.

High Halden was luckier than many parishes in the area to come out of the Second World War relatively unscathed in material terms. But it lost loved ones, experienced horrors and displayed much resourcefulness and bravery nonetheless. As such, it represents the best of a Kentish village during these times – steadfast and undaunted, even while the mightiest foe in recorded history was throwing all it could at it.

THE END

PUBLISHER'S NOTE

For the sake of clarity and reasons of space it has been decided not to include endnote references. Any reader wishing for expansion or elucidation on any points in this book is invited to contact the author via the publisher at **info@canterley.co.uk**

INDEX

Follow us on Twitter or Facebook
for news on the latest publications.

www.canterley.co.uk